Tipsy in Madras

Tipsy
in
Madras

A Complete Guide to 80s Preppy Drinking, Including
Proper Attire, Cocktails for Every Occasion, the
Best Beer, the Right Mixers, and More!

MATT "JOHNNIE" WALKER & MARISSA "MITZY" WALSH

A PERIGEE BOOK

A Perigee Book
Published by The Berkley Publishing Group
A division of Penguin Group (USA) Inc.
375 Hudson Street
New York, New York 10014

Copyright © 2004 by Matt Walker
and Marissa Walsh
Cover design by Ben Gibson
Text design by Richard Oriolo

First Perigee paperback edition: May 2003

Visit our website at www.penguin.com

LIBRARY OF CONGRESS CATALOGING-IN-PUBLICATION DATA

Walker, Matt, 1972–
    Tipsy in Madras: a complete guide to 80s preppy drinking / Matt "Johnnie" Walker & Marissa "Mitzy" Walsh.—1st ed.
        p. cm.
    Includes bibliographical references.
    ISBN 0-399-52985-3
    1. Cocktails. I. Walsh, Marissa, 1973– II. Title.

TX951.W274 2004
641.8'74—dc22

                                                        2003066044

Printed in the United States of America

10   9   8   7   6   5   4   3   2   1

For our parents,

for agreeing to send us to prep school

but *not* boarding school

"A Yale man gets drunk in a wholly different way from a Penn State man."

—DWIGHT MACDONALD

CONTENTS

APPENDICES

See Ya Later, Alligator
(In a While, Crocodile):
How "Party" Became a Verb

"So you play the clarinet, huh, Steve?" Mr. Cartwright began.

"Yes, I do," Stephen answered. He hesitated slightly before he spoke again. "Uhm, I like to be called Stephen, not Steve. I'm not very fond of nicknames. A little too preppy for my tastes."

Now Missy's cheeks began to burn and she turned toward Stephen, who had sat down in the rocking chair near the fireplace. "And what's wrong with being a preppy?" she asked him sharply.

—STEPHANIE AUSTIN, *THE PREPPY PROBLEM* (1984)

Why preppy drinks? Why the 1980s? Why preppy drinks of the 1980s?

We can explain.

Preppies no longer exist.

You read right. Oh, you might think you know preppies, and you probably do. That is, you know relatively "preppy" people. But preppies *as a class* became extinct about twenty years ago. You might find this claim incredible. Preppies are a venerable breed, you might think. We wouldn't necessarily dispute you. They'd had their time in the country-club sun before: the 1920s, the 1950s. To fulfill the thirty-year cycle, they returned again in the early 1980s. For a brief madras moment, it looked like pink and green would last forever.

Set the Way-Back Machine to the late-seventies. It was an age of Farrah Fawcett–feathered folly, Harvey Wallbanger–fueled key parties, and est-ian excess. Signs of revolt against Dacron were imminent, however. And that revolt rightly came from the graduates of the nation's prep schools. In 1979, Nelson W. Aldrich, Jr., wrote a cover story for *The Atlantic* entitled "Preppies: The Last Upper Class?" Preppy style seemed the era's last best hope for ending the nation's long leisure-suited nightmare. If they were in fact the last upper class it was the least they could do to fulfill their sense of noblesse oblige.

By the spring of 1980, the fashion rags were predicting that "the preppy look" would be hot for the fall. Before the summer even began, G.H. Bass & Co. upped the production number on Weejuns to 6,000 pairs daily. (An Atlanta shoe saleswoman told *Time*, "If one more person comes in here and asks for Bass Weejuns, I think I'll scream.") Then, in November 1980 came *The Official Preppy Handbook*. Conceived by Jonathan Roberts and edited by Lisa Birnbach it became the Little Plaid Book for the cultural counterrevolution. From the 40,000 copy first printing, its publisher shipped a mere 24,000 copies to bookstores. By the end of the year, however, 550,000 copies were in print; within a year, the book would sell more than a million copies and reach #1 on bestseller lists across the land.

Eighties prep had its distinct flavor. You could see it in movies like *Class, St. Elmo's Fire, Private School (for Girls), Oxford Blues, Trading Places,* and yes, *Preppies*. Meanwhile, television shows like *The Facts of Life, Family Ties, Kate and Allie,* and *Diff'rent Strokes* all were "prepped" for prime time. Face it: When else could George Plimpton have hawked home video game systems? In some towns, you could even "Rent-a-Prep" to do your lawn work and paint your house. You never knew what pastel shade you'd end up with. It was a frenzy of mallards and Muffys.

The backlash was inevitable, however. It began with titles like *The I-Hate-Preppies Handbook* and *Save an Alligator, Shoot a Preppy*. College-age entrepreneurs cranked out antipreppy buttons. Movies like *Alligator* demonized the preppy mascot and every movie starring James Spader demonized the preppy himself.

THE SHIRT

"The crocodile, not alligator, please. I was known as Le Crocodile." —RENE LACOSTE

Those sherbet-colored shirts with the famous emblem were required wear (with collars up, natch) for any prep worth his or her tennis game in the '80s. But was the emblem an alligator or a crocodile? Depends on which translator you ask.

The shirt was invented by French tennis champion Rene "Le Crocodile" Lacoste, who earned his nickname because of his ferocity on the tennis court. He took to his nickname so much that he soon began wearing the crocodile on his tennis clothing—a great way to psych out an opponent! In 1933, he decided to offer his crocodile-embroidered short-sleeved white cotton shirts to the public. In 1951, Lacoste partnered

Backlash aside, the preppies had already sensed that their position was tenuous. The high-prep era correlates roughly with the first term of Ronald Reagan's presidency—1980 to 1984. Although Nancy put hard alcohol back on the White House drink menu, "The Gipper" himself was hardly a preppy. Not only was he from California, he wore tacky brown suits, ate jelly beans, and had worked in *show business*. Consequently, preppies considered their own doom with a special sense of acuteness. Downward social mobility was always a lurking possibility; and as the with IZOD and introduced color and pique knit shirts. They began exporting the shirts to the United States a year later. And perhaps that is when "the crocodile" got lost in the translation. Everyone referred to the reptile on the shirts as *an alligator*. The difference? The alligator's snout is broad, the croc's is narrow; the former summers in Palm Beach, the latter in "The Islands."

Alas, the Lacoste-IZOD partnership ended in 1993, and Lacoste reentered the United State market on its own in 1996. "I suppose you could say that if it had been a really nice animal, something sympathetic, then maybe nothing would have happened," Lacoste once reportedly remarked. "Suppose I had picked a rooster. Well, that's French, but it doesn't have the same impact." We also have Lacoste to thank for the first steel tennis racket.

preppies in Whit Stillman's *Metropolitan* came to realize, each debutante season could be the last.

Doom and obsolescence. The theme would show up in the unlikeliest places. Consider the following exchange:

"But if you're preppy you don't get laid in a car."
"Where you get laid if you preppy?"
I sniffed. "One doesn't," I said.
"Preppies gonna be outnumbered in a while," Hawk said.

—ROBERT B. PARKER (COLBY '54), *CEREMONY* (1982)

Indeed, Reagan's election was the seed that would blossom with poisoned fruit only a few years later. The December 31, 1984, issue of *Newsweek* confirmed everyone's worst suspicions: It was officially "The Year of the Yuppie." The preppy locomotive, powered by gentleman's Cs and frayed khakis, had reached its last stop; the yuppie's American Express would soon overtake it. The earliest observers of the shift could tell the difference between the old guard and the upstarts. Yet the misconception gradually spread that yuppies were just late-model preppies. As Michael Lewis's *Liar's Poker* noted, more than a few preppy Princeton grads happened to be driven econ majors hungry for analyst slots at Salomon Brothers. Yuppie, preppy: People are suckers for rhyming words. Things were bound to get confused.

With the arrival of the yuppie, the rules changed. Love of the worn, the known, the convivial, was replaced by a competitive cosmopolitanism that would eventually spawn that great cocktail of the 1990s, the cosmopolitan. At the bar, simple was out, while Japanese liqueurs, weird mixers, and name-brand logos were in with a vengeance. Whiskey and scotch were over; vodka of every conceivable variety was *now*. In fact, the popularity of vodka—the alcohol that aspires to the condition of water—spoke volumes. Yuppies were never entirely comfortable with drinking itself: workaholism trumped alcoholism, and better to get a stress fracture at the health club or file overtime than drink a drop. It was no coincidence that the national drinking age shot up from eighteen to twenty-one by mid-decade. (It no longer mattered that the governor of preppy Vermont opposed the law.)

Confronted with yupsthetes wielding shiny Italian designer accessories and an encyclopedic knowledge of world cuisine, what could the preppy do? The choice was clear: either join in the orgy or cast oneself willfully into obscurity. Always seeking a reasonable compromise, preps did both. The ones who didn't just retire to the Connecticut countryside adopted Ralph (Lifshitz) Lauren's ersatz "classic" stylings, both in clothing and spirit. And so, in a few short years, the boom went bust and the drinking customs that preps had maintained and passed down for decades found themselves disappearing forever.

By the start of the nineties, the collapse of the American stock market and a wave of insider trading and S&L scandals spelled the end of the yuppie moment. Nevertheless, those young urban professionals would maintain a gold-plated grip on public perception of the preceding decade. People forgot about the preppies and especially about what they drank. Ask someone today what a classic preppy drink of the 1980s was, chances are they'll respond, "screaming banana orgasm" or "sex on the beach."

Such ignorance is inexcusable.

That's where we come in.

We attended prep schools in the 1980s. We know the preppy beast—sometimes too well. Our method, such as it is, can be described as speculative archeology. We've scoured classic preppy books—both fiction and nonfiction—from the 1980s and before. We've reviewed and analyzed the great preppy films of the decade, our eyes always on the liquor cabinet. And when we've been left only with fragmentary evidence, we've relied on memory, interviews, and well-honed guesswork to fill in the gaps. The result, we think, is the most comprehensive account of preppy '80s drinking that anyone could ever formulate.

Along the way, we've had to come to grips with the slippery nature of preppiness itself. Preps may be good cocktail party conversationalists, witty persons "of character," but not the most self-reflective people. The prep is a creature of inherited customs and traditions: The true prep doesn't need to follow a handbook; he just follows in Father's footsteps. Despite this informality, every aspect of prep school life is governed by the most explicit rules and principles, which are spelled out in each year's catalog. Therein lies the preppy paradox. No wonder he needs a drink; but how does he choose it?

Here, then, are a few guidelines to keep in mind as you join us on our booze-geois adventure:

1. **AVAILABILITY**: A preppy drink of the 1980s was readily available *in* the 1980s. Cosmopolitans were not widely available until the 1990s. They were not drinks that Bootsy enjoyed, even if they are drinks that Charlotte now might.

2. **ARCHAISM**: The preppy drink existed *before* the 1980s. As with prep school traditions, as with preppy clothing, as with preppy drinks: Affinity for the old makes preppies suspicious of novelty and undue trendiness. That is not to say that on occasion they won't indulge in the Now; but for them, the Classic usually is Now.

3. **CHARACTER**: Prep schools are crucibles of pain that eschew the cheap and the easy. Thus, unlike the general American population, which enjoys soft

drinks and cocktails that aspire to the condition of soft drinks, preps enjoy drinks that function as tests of character. Thus, the prevalence of straight alcohol, bitters, and dryness as filtering devices; thus also, the prevalence of high alcohol content as a test to determine whether one is a "lightweight"—that is, whether one has sufficient self-control to maintain composure and invincibility in the face of sheer drunkenness.

4. ARCHAIC PRIORITY: In cases of conflict, Archaism maintains priority over Character. Preps may choose sweet drinks, provided they pick drinks approved by the Principle of Archaism; thus, the sour and the Collins, which have been around for decades, are acceptable; drinks with crass sexual connotations (e.g., the sloe comfortable screw and the blow job) are not.

5. UNDERSTATEMENT: The preppy drink is there to be drunk, not to be advertised. It keeps a low profile and lifts its eyebrow at showiness. Thus, while preppy drinks may have garnishes, the garnish is minimal—a lime wedge, an olive, an onion. Likewise, the preppy drink does not rely on any "name" brand of alcohol. Its surface appearance often gives no indication as to just what it is.

6. EFFICIENCY: As a corollary of the Principles of Character and Understatement: From the minimum possible bar comes the maximum number of

preppy drinks; the drink with the fewest ingredients is the preppiest. And if one follows the advice of Kingsley Amis in his classic, *On Drink*, a bigger drink is preppier than a smaller one. "Serious drinkers will be pleased and reassured, unserious ones will not be offended, and you will use up less chatting-time going round to recharge glasses."

7. ANGLICANISM: The prep school, as an American adoption of the British public school, is rooted in the Anglican tradition. So, too, are preppy drinks. Hence, gin and whiskey are preppiest; rum and vodka *are* preppy, though slightly less so. Midori and Green Apple Schnapps are definitely *not* preppy. The more "exotic" a drink is, the less preppy it is. If a drink relies on a colorful form of alcohol generally available only post-1980, it is apt to be yuppie; if it relies on one available pre-1980, it is apt to be a prep drink only for slummin'.

8. CARELESSNESS: The preppy drink is not a feat of high engineering. Getting the proportions right is often not a matter of precision, but of trial and error. Like the hastily tied bow tie or the tweed jacket missing a button, a careful carelessness reveals that the prep is unbound to common propriety.

In sum:

• Would Blair Warner drink it on a "very special" episode of *The Facts of Life*?

THE PREPPY TOP TEN

For those readers who relied on Monarch Notes during their adolescent years, here's a list to get started. Just don't drink them all at once.

1. Bloody Mary
2. Gin and tonic
3. Scotch (neat or with water)
4. Cape Codder
5. Old-fashioned

6. Dry martini
7. Gimlet
8. Manhattan
9. Rum and tonic
10. Planters Punch

- Would James "Steff" Spader drink it at his party in *Pretty in Pink*?

- Would your grandfather drink it?

The early 1980s were the ultimate heyday of preppiness. But last call came too soon for preppy drinking. Set 'em up Joe: We're back.

The Authors

Prepping the Bar:
Stock Options

"The Proper Philadelphian walks where other Americans would ride, and rarely takes a taxi; he lives within his income and never spends principal; favors an automobile of any color as long as it is black (whitewall tires); talks a great deal about how little, rather than how much, he paid for this and that, and never mentions what he is worth. He is, in effect, affirming his faith in the 'Spartan-Puritan' virtues."

—E. DIGBY BALTZELL, *PHILADELPHIA GENTLEMEN* (1958)

There's a lot of mythology about what constitutes a bar. One group obsesses and fusses over every detail, thinking that if you don't have all the right glasses, spirits, and accoutrements, you belong in a zoo. Indeed, fearful of slipping up, this subpopulation is really the only one that talks about "spirits" in the first place; to say "booze" would be to risk being confused with the *Married with Children* set. Just as they memorize "dress for global domination" manuals, this group takes great pains to present respectability, but the sheer effort required shows up like the all-too-neatly pressed shine of their Oxford shirts. In reaction to such silliness, another group rails against it all with a grumble and sticks to cans of Pabst.

As an upholder of the Golden Mean, however, the seasoned prep steers an even course between a prickly refinement on one hand, and a vulgar excess on the other. Keeping with this sensibility, the preppy bar is at once tasteful and unencumbered with nonsense. Like a decent preppy wardrobe, such a bar thumbs its nose at the vagaries of fashion, just as it reveals a certain ragged elegance. Again, the yuppie/preppy distinction puts matters into relief: the yuppie will head immediately for Williams-Sonoma and Dean & DeLuca in a tizzy, while the preppy trades in what is passed-down through the generations, what is extra in the summer house, what has been pilfered from one's prep school or college dining hall, the country club, or from the alumni clubs of rival universities. The key is durability and practicality. To dispel any illusions about just what this requires, however, we present the following general guidelines. As with all guidelines in this book, we offer them as useful rules of thumb distilled (as it were) from the rough and tumble of preppy practice; they are not intended as computer programs to run on your vintage Apple IIe.

Bar None: Booze to Keep on Hand

When it comes to deliberating about the booze with which to stock one's bar, the diffusion of yuppie pride has led to

BAR? PREPPY? PREPPY BAR?: THINGS TO LOOK FOR WHEN DRINKING AWAY FROM HOME

- Preponderance of wooden fixtures
- Located in an old hotel
- Dress code in effect
- Banquette
- Male bartender of a certain age who doesn't need to look up drink recipes
- Studded upholstery on leather chairs
- Celery stalks at ready

much unnecessary confusion and hand-wringing. By contrast, preps pick the right booze in the right way: steering through the liquor store aisles with good sense and an estimate of everything's value, they avoid brands that commit the vice of excess (i.e., gaudiness and trendiness), as well as the vice of deficiency (i.e., sheer gut-rottiness). House brands should not be overlooked.

ONE BOTTLE GIN: Gilbey's and Gordon's are preppy; Bombay and Bombay Sapphire are yuppie. Depending on context, Tanqueray and Beefeater *can* be preppy in virtue of their *haute* Anglo stylings, though their price usually screams yuppie.

ONE BOTTLE SCOTCH: Dewar's and J&B are preppy; Chivas Regal is yuppie.

ONE BOTTLE BOURBON/TENNESSEE WHISKEY: Jack Daniel's and Jim Beam are preppy; Maker's Mark and Knob Creek are yuppie.

ONE BOTTLE CANADIAN WHISKEY: Canadian Club is preppy; Crown Royal and Seagram's V.O. are yuppie.

ONE BOTTLE VODKA: Gilbey's, Smirnoff, and Gordon's are preppy; Absolut, Skyy, Stolichnaya, and Ketel One are yuppie.

ONE BOTTLE RUM: Mount Gay and Bacardi are preppy; Plantation is yuppie.

ONE BOTTLE DRY VERMOUTH, ONE BOTTLE SWEET VERMOUTH: Martini and Rossi's often the only game in town.

Finally, you will need one case of beer and one bottle each of red wine and white wine. See chapter 3, "Do Brahmins Drink Budweiser?" and chapter 8, "The Wrath of Grapes," respectively, for more specific comments.

NOTE: Preps always buy the big bottle, not the little one.

The Second Round: Other Bottles to Have on Hand

Like a good prep school education, the following extra items make you (and your bar) well-rounded. Of course, circumstances and recipes will require other liquors, but the following will help you cover the bulk of the drinks discussed in this book. Unless otherwise noted, go for the house brand.

One bottle coffee liquor (e.g., Kahlúa)
One bottle triple sec
One bottle tequila
One bottle brandy
One bottle Pernod

Completing the Bar

While there is something to be said for straight up or on the rocks, you'll need a few other items to round out the bar. Happily, you can find them all in the beverage aisle of your local grocery store.

THE LIQUOR STORE ACCOUNT

Preps typically try to avoid having to deal with cash: Financial matters are best kept discreet, of course. Thus, they keep accounts with a good local liquor store. While fewer liquor stores these days are willing to grant this special kind of credit, a liquor account can be passed down like an old cardigan: thus, Taylor III gets started on Taylor II's account, and eventually takes it over. Internet booze merchants offer accounts these days, but the Internet is not preppy. If you don't have an account at your local liquor merchant, you might inquire into getting one—especially if you're a regular. Bonus points if you can get them to deliver.

MIXERS AND CONDIMENTS

Sour mix (Mr. & Mrs. T)
Lemon juice
Lime juice (Rose's)
Grenadine (Rose's)
Bitters (Angostura, orange)
Sugar (superfine granulated)
Salt (kosher rock, not table)

NOTE: If you're serving Bloodies, you'll need a few extra condiments; see chapter 6, "The Sun's Past Half-Mast."

JUICES

Grapefruit juice   Orange juice

Cranberry juice   Tomato juice

SOFT DRINKS AND WATERS

(For more information, see Chapter 9, "Taking the Waters.")

Cola   Club soda

Ginger ale   Tonic water

Seltzer water   Perrier

GARNISHES

Lemon and lime slices

Green olives (plain is preppier than with pimiento)

Maraschino cherries

UTENSILS

BLENDER: Necessary for frozen drinks and crushing ice—usually more for the latter. Go with classic chrome.

BOTTLE OPENER: Typically, preps carry these around on their key chains. Generally, they picked them up as freebies during their college years, when the breakup of AT&T led various companies to flock to campuses, trying to interest preps in phone service. That was before cell phones took over; of course, as good traditionalists, preppies don't like to use cell phones.

CAN OPENER: Useful for canned fruit juice. Preps usually just buy their fruit juice in cartons or bottles, but

SHAKERS FOR QUAKERS
(AND OTHER SIDWELL FRIENDS)

Old-time mixologists make fine-tuned distinctions among the various types of cocktail shakers now available on the market. While most professional bartenders (e.g., *Cocktail*'s Tom Cruise and Bryan Brown) use the Boston shaker—a sixteen-ounce steel tumbler and twelve-ounce thick-walled glass tumbler—the classic three-part shaker is to be preferred. The classic shaker consists of a metal tumbler, a lid, and a cap that fits over the lid and covers a built-in strainer. You can buy these new at stores like Crate & Barrel.

The cobalt blue glass models produced in the 1930s by Washington, Pennsylvania's Hazel Atlas Glass Company—which come decorated with fish, sailboats, and golfers—are among the preppiest. So too are

one never knows when one will need the pineapple, yes? Use the handheld, triangular puncture model that doubles as a bottle opener, not the electric.

CORKSCREW: Forget about the Eurostyle air-pump models and stick with the classic "worm" spiral style.

COCKTAIL SHAKER: See "Shakers for Quakers (and other Sidwell Friends)," above.

CUTTING BOARD: Use this to cut lime and lemon wedges for your classics. While the social-climbing yuppie goes for marble, the true prep goes for wood.

shakers with rooster imprints. (Cocktail—get it?) While 1950s shakers imprinted with atom designs have a certain charm, they are not as preppy as the shakers from the post-Prohibition golden age of 1933 to 1941. Nowadays, though, the older shakers are pricey collectors items: collectible dealer Dan Walker tells us that one can expect to shell out about $95 on average for a Hazel Atlas shaker; some of the more obscure designs sell for a few hundred or more.

BASIC SHAKER TECHNIQUE

Pour your ingredients into the metal container and add ice cubes. Secure your lid and cap, and shake for ten seconds. Remove the cap and strain the contents into your glass.

ICE BUCKET: A good ice bucket will have room for at least three trays of ice cubes. Or keep a ten-pound bag of ice in the freezer and refill the bucket as necessary.

ICE TONGS: In a pinch, you can always just use your hands, but tongs keep things neat.

JIGGER: This is essentially a measuring cup to let you know how much booze you're pouring in. Jiggers are usually double-ended, one side typically holding one ounce, the other holding one and a half ounces. Or just use a shot glass.

KNIFE: Keep one of these on hand to cut lime and lemon wedges. A paring knife does the trick.

SPOON: To stir drinks and to measure small amounts, use a tablespoon.

STRAINER: This helpful utensil fits over a shaker or mixing glass to prevent unsightly chunks of ice from falling into your martini. (Hint: The classic cocktail shaker comes with one of these; that's why it's classic.)

THERMOS: One of the few great inventions of the Space Age. Mix up some Bloody Marys (see chapter 6, "The Sun's Past Half-Mast") and put them into this delightful contraption for a picnic brunch. Underage boarding school preps have long been known to use these to psych out clueless housemasters.

TOWEL: Cotton only, for cleaning up spills. Pub towels add a certain touch of charm.

WASTEPAPER BASKET: If you line a clean one with a plastic garbage bag, you can use it for mixing up a fierce punch. You can also keep one on hand for those without a due sense of their own limits. Or you can use it for trash.

PRESENTATION SUPPLIES

COASTERS: Keep some on hand to prevent your tables from suffering water damage. Go with mallard prints.

COCKTAIL NAPKINS: Gingham and plaid are good. See the caveat (in "The Flask") concerning monograms.

SWIZZLE STICKS: Keep them simple, or better yet, take a few from your favorite hotel bar.

DON'T BOTHER WITH . . .

BOTTLE POURERS: Professional bartenders use these, but preppiness is all about amateurism in the classical sense. Indeed, uncapped bottles pour pretty well on their own. (And please, no fancy bottle-tossing tricks.)

COCKTAIL PICKS: These exist to support garnishes. Aside for the simple lime wedge or olive, however, preppy drinks are aggressively garnish-free, so you don't need cocktail picks. Flashy garnishes are tacky; save the little umbrellas for the tiki bar.

FRUIT JUICERS: As some wag once observed, only Californians have lifestyles. Likewise, only Californians drink fresh-squeezed juice. Preps go for cartons or bottles, usually Tropicana.

THE FLASK

An essential component of the preppy bar-on-the-go, and popular Prohibition-era accoutrement, the flask turns any event into a party.

WHAT ARE THEY MADE OF? Many flasks are made of one metal, e.g., silver, stainless steel, chrome, or pewter. Some flasks use one of these metals, but are leather-covered. Others feature custom-made leather case coverings. Silver and pewter are good preppy picks. Chrome and stainless also work.

HOW MUCH DO THEY CARRY? A small flask will carry around three ounces. Average hip flasks carry anywhere between five and eight ounces.

HOW MUCH DO THEY COST? Prices start at around $20 to $25.00 for a basic stainless steel model, and average about $45 to $50.00 for an ostrich leather–covered or top grade stainless. Pewter can go for a little more—$40 to $80.00—but preps consider such flasks sound investments.

WHERE CAN YOU BUY THEM? Tobacco stores and travel supply stores stock a wide range of models.

GOOD PICKS: The hip flask, boot flask, and round flask all have tradition in their favor. As their names suggest, a hip flask is carried in one's front pocket, while a boot flask slips into one's boot. Such models—which one typically imagines when one thinks of "flasks"—tend also to be easily concealed. Round flasks fit in your pocket, though some attach to your belt.

BAD PICKS: A tower flask will carry up to around ten ounces, is seven inches tall, and comes with two cups. Only James Bond villains would use one of these. Stick with the Thermos. Similarly, imprint flasks (with Jack Daniel's and New York Yankees logos) are out, as are avant-garde flasks, such as oval flasks and flasks in weird geometrical shapes. Finally, flasks with custom-designed leather covers with little pictures of dragonflies and such are both tacky and expensive; expect to shell out $300.00 or so for one of these specimens of fisherman kitsch.

TO MONOGRAM OR NOT TO MONOGRAM?: Contrary to a popular misconception fostered by *The Official Preppy Handbook*, preps don't monogram everything; only amnesiacs do. Monograms *in principle* are okay, provided they're done in moderation. Always acceptable is something old monogrammed to somebody else, typically an eccentric great uncle or aunt, which you then inherit. But in sum, the decision to monogram is a matter of individual conscience and good judgment, though one runs one's risks in adding initials carelessly.

An *engraved* gift flask, of course, is always okay. For romance, you can't beat:

> "To 1st Lt. F. Scott Fitzgerald
> 65th Infantry
> Camp Sheridan
>
> Forget-me-not
> Zelda
> 9-13-18
> Montgomery, Ala"

GLASSWARE

For godssakes, keep it *simple*. While one can pour one's drinks into over a dozen different kinds of glasses—Irish coffee glasses, margarita glasses, sour glasses—all the preppy bartender needs are the following:

COCKTAIL GLASS: The *V*-shaped glass is essential for serving martinis and related drinks. In his book *Martini, Straight Up*, author Lowell Edmunds points out that while the modern martini glass came unto its own in the late 1920s, prototypes appeared in the 1870s, and glasses with cone-shaped bowls showed up in Italy as early as the late 1600s.

COLLINS GLASS: A narrow, eight- to twelve-ounce tumbler. Good for Collins drinks, obviously, but will do the trick for highballs, beers, and sodas.

OLD-FASHIONED GLASS: Good for *anything* on the rocks. Heavy and oversized, it makes for a nice paperweight to boot. A medium five- to ten-ounce tumbler.

PINT GLASS: A fourteen- to sixteen-ounce tumbler for beer.

SHOT GLASS: A miniature tumbler that holds one to two ounces. These are useful for measuring, as well as for birthday shots.

WINEGLASS: These typically hold five to ten ounces. Red-wine glasses have a wider bowl and larger lip than those meant for white wine, but either will do the job.

While the above glass selection is a pretty spartan arrangement no matter how you look at it, some catering types insist that one can always pare down even further. As an all-purpose glass, the stem goblet, which holds twelve ounces, is recommended. While adherence to the goblet-or-bust rule eliminates the idiosyncrasy that makes a bar truly preppy, it can keep things simple if the party's going to be large. The goblets also leave fewer ring stains on furniture. Use your best judgment.

ON THE ROAD

Don't be limited in your barware. There's a certain charm to serving highballs in the family china and kamikazes in coffee mugs. And don't forget the "roadie," the insulated plastic "to-go" cup, useful when your guests want to imbibe in the car and you don't want to send your glassware with them. (Of course, the roadie is appropriate for passengers only.)

A note on plastic: If you're throwing either a kegger or a party near a body of water (e.g., on a beach or next to a swimming pool), disposable plastic cups are acceptable.

Where to Find Vintage Preppy Drinking Supplies

Preps keep faithful to their old school. While they prefer the unadorned, they will undoubtedly have at least one school logo drinking item on hand. Glasses with prep school logos are usually only available from the school itself. Buying these can be tricky, since one often has to be a current student with an account. Moreover, since private schools cater to an underage crowd, one is unlikely to find much more than a mug or plastic cup. Aside from the opportunities that the occasional alumni reunion can afford, one should keep one's eyes peeled for prep school benefit flea markets, which are typically held in the spring. One can usually find a few interesting surprises on the cluttered tables of battered skiing equipment and old handbags. Prep school athletic prize mugs always go well with a Löwenbräu.

More plentiful and useful, however, are preppy college seal mugs and glasses from college bookstores and off-campus stationery stores. While these establishments are often warehouses of gold-plated alumni kitsch aimed at the B-schoolers, the basic models are often the best. Virtually all colleges and universities these days belong to the Independent Labeling Program, which stamps officially licensed goods with the red, white, and blue Collegiate Licensed Products sticker. Some of the larger licensees include American Decorators in Lansdale, Pennsylvania, and the Nordic Company in Riverside, Rhode Island. The typography used on mugs and glassware typically changes about once every decade or so, with blockier typefaces used in the 1970s and thinner "neo-classical" typefaces in the 1980s and 1990s.

Beer tankards with Gothic or block "collegiate" typefaces stay the same for generations, yet the benefits of their durability must be balanced against their characteristic clunkiness.

The prep who cares about these things will go for the really old stuff. On ebay.com and at antique stores in college

ALMA MATER

While the Ivies and the Seven Sisters are traditionally preppy (though to varying degrees—cf. Penn and Barnard), some smaller colleges actually attract preppier students. No matter where you go, you're bound to drink.

THE IVIES: Brown, Columbia, Cornell, Dartmouth, Harvard, University of Pennsylvania, Princeton, and Yale

THE POTTED IVIES: Amherst, Wesleyan, Williams

THE SEVEN SISTERS: Barnard, Bryn Mawr, Mount Holyoke, Radcliffe, Smith, Vassar, Wellesley

THE PREPPIES: Babson, Bates, Bowdoin, Colby, Colorado College, Connecticut College, Denison, Georgetown, Hamilton, Hollins University (neé College), Lake Forest, Middlebury, St. Lawrence, Sweet Briar, Trinity (Conn.), University of Virginia, Washington and Lee, Wheaton towns, one can find mugs and glassware going all the way back to around 1900. Another popular destination is Brimfield, Massachusetts, right in the heart of prep school territory and home to the nation's biggest flea markets in May, July, and September. (See "Mail Order: Preppy Drinking Suppliers" for more information.) Look out for china with spiffy scrollwork and archaic versions of school seals. Better-living-through-Bauhaus design was common in the 1950s and 1960s; still, some of the renditions of school mascots from this era can be quite charming. Finally, keep your eyes out for collectible models from the "Harvard Cooperative Society" and the now-defunct Yale Coop.

If, however, you want something new, or if you need new replacements after breaking your old goods at a raucous soiree, you'll need to go the college store route. As one might expect, the selection and variety of drinking supplies varies according to the school. There's nothing to do but drink in godforsaken Williamstown, Massachusetts; thus the prodigious collection of mugs and glasses at the Williams Shop. At the Sweet Briar Book Shop, one can find champagne flutes with silk-screened college seals. Yet given the beer-addled reputations of students at Big Green, there's a surprisingly small selection of drinking items at the Dartmouth Coop. You don't need to be a Harvard alum to drink out of a Harvard tankard. (See "Mail Order: Preppy Drinking Suppliers" for store information.)

And A Final Word . . .

Don't forget the pretzels and salted peanuts. Store brand will do. And don't be tempted by the Pepperidge Farm Goldfish.

Summering:
Drinking Light in
Tennis White

"If Audrey's supposed to be visiting Cynthia in Connecticut, and Cynthia's with Von Sloneker in Southampton—what does that mean? There's only one explanation—Audrey's gone with Cynthia to Von Sloneker's 'house party' in Southampton!"

—TOM, IN *METROPOLITAN* (1990)

Summering. Drinking. Summering and drinking. For the prep, the two words are synonymous from Memorial Day to Labor Day. Whether at the beach or in the "country" (i.e., suburban Connecticut), on the tennis court or on the yacht, there's a drink for every activity. Drinking opportunities abound. Like the madras Bermuda shorts and sundresses favored by preps this time of year, the prep summer drink is light and colorful. It makes a fine accessory. So take off your socks and pass the gin.

The Fresh Air Trust Fund

For preps, the tradition of summering begins in the formative years. Most private schools dismiss their pupils in May, so the prep summer begins Memorial Day weekend and ends Labor Day weekend. In addition to the four-bedroom Colonial or pre-war Fifth Avenue apartment called home, every prep family maintains a summer house, usually in the country or by the sea. While Mum and Father play gin rummy and sip gin and tonics, their prep offspring learn to appreciate nautical motifs, such as anchors and whales. (Australian au pairs are helpful in this regard.) The children learn to sail and annoy Mummy by insisting on wearing knotted fishermen's rope bracelets until they get dirty and ragged and eventually fall off. For inland preps, summer's all about the club. At the golf and tennis/country club the young prep pup can take tennis, golf, and swimming lessons. No matter the pastime, summer marks itself off as a special, enchanted time. Days are longer. Nights chirp with cicadas. The surrounding is different, and normal rules and rigid dress codes do not apply.

As prep children grow older, however, it's time for them to get in the family's weekend Volvo station wagon and learn the prep virtue of responsibility. And so they're packed off from the family's summer house for an even more authentic summer (July) experience: camp. While Emerson had his proto-hippie trappings, he did go to Harvard. And if he could learn self-reliance in the woods, so too can George Jr., and Bitsy. Summer camps, idyllic spaces named after imaginary indigenous tribes, are characteristically located someplace wooded—usually in New England, though a few well-established camps thrive in Pennsylvania and New York.

At camp, the prep child undergoes an important rite of passage. After so many summers of fluorescent Kool-Aid "bug juice," it's time for something with a little kick. Inevitably, sympathetic camp counselors—usually old camp alums themselves—will sneak in a cheap bottle of tipple for the younger. One might think the counselors are corrupting the youth, but in their role as seasoned guides, the elders are merely transmitting an older code of aristocratic values. Like an old walking stick or a fine Shetland sweater, an important prep tradition is passed down to the next generation.

If the growing prep is too old for summer camp or is building a boat that summer instead, the summerhouse also affords the opportunity for a baptismal inbibation. In the adolescent years, the beach house becomes a fine place to catch up on *The Catcher in the Rye* or another required prep school summer reading title (see box). As sun sets, though, it's time for a bonfire, clambake, and drink on the sand.

3. *The Old Man and the Sea* by Ernest Hemingway
   The marlin that got away.

4. *The Great Gatsby* by F. Scott Fitzgerald
   The Donald.

5. *Lord of the Flies* by William Golding
   Nasty, brutish, and short.

6. *The Chosen* by Chaim Potok
   Mandatory.

7. *Ethan Frome* by Edith Wharton
   Nag, nag, nag.

8. *Slaughterhouse-Five* by Kurt Vonnegut
   Pilgrim's progress.

9. *Pigeon Feathers and Other Stories* by John Updike
   His stepson went to my prep school.

10. *To Kill a Mockingbird* by Harper Lee
    One-hit wonder.

SIGNING BONUS

As prep youth matures, the pleasures of summering are not easily forgotten. Prep professions keep to the time-honored rule of "work hard, play hard." Summer hours (9 to 5:45 Monday through Thursday; 9 to 1 on Friday) afford ample opportunity to get to the family's summer escape. Guests are always welcome, of course, as long as they bring a bottle and a knack for badminton. For the younger prep who in-

MINT JULEP: GO, BABY, GO!

The Mint Julep is not technically a summer drink. It's a first-Saturday-in-May drink, which is when the Kentucky Derby is run every year. Conveniently, this is also when the drink's key ingredient—mint—is in bloom. More than 2,000 pounds of freshly harvested mint is served in Derby Mint Juleps each year.

While hats and horses are acceptable at other times of the year, you'll be relieved to know Mint Juleps are not. Making simple syrup the night before is a lot to go through for an event that only lasts two minutes! But, once a year, it's worth it.

2 OZ. BOURBON

1 TBSP. SIMPLE SYRUP

10–15 LARGE FRESH MINT LEAVES

Make a simple syrup by boiling two cups each of sugar and water together for five minutes. Cool and place in a covered container with six or eight sprigs of fresh mint and refrigerate overnight.

Mash mint leaves and simple syrup with the back of a silver spoon in the bottom of a glass. (Ideally a silver cup or mug, if you've got one lying around.) Fill glass with crushed ice and add bourbon. Garnish with mint sprig. Collect your winnings.

sists on shunning tradition, there is always the summer share in the Hamptons (a.k.a. The Paco Rabanne Factory Outlet). Mum may say it's gauche, Biff from his Groton days may accuse him of slumming, but where else is he going to meet Bo Derek? Don't worry, he'll be back to his senses and Blair come October.

As the summering adult prep soon learns, a well-mixed drink makes life easier. Who growing up in the '80s thought that we would have to work this hard?

AUTUMN

By now, the prep has inherited the family's summer compound or bought one of her own. She will have bred and her children will attend the same summer camp and swim in the same ocean that she did. As she gets old, she may extend her stay at the summerhouse. She may actually begin to prefer mid-September when all the summer people have gone. But she will never wear white after Labor Day except on the squash or tennis court. As the autumn leaves rustle their first, her bar is still stocked; and despite the coming of earlier sunsets, there's always time for one of these light drinks.

Summer People: Gin Drinks

Gin was first created in Holland in the 17th century by one Doctor Sylvius (a.k.a. Franciscus de la Boe). With Cartesian flourish, the good doctor deduced that a distilled spirit made from grain and flavored with juniper would be medically useful. Straight gin is almost intolerably nasty, and so his conclusions made some sense, at least in the sense that "foul taste" = "medically useful." The British called Sylvius's concoction "Dutch courage," and they guzzled it in great quantities during the Thirty Years War. By the time Queen Anne reigned over the British Isles, the British discovered how to produce gin themselves; "London Dry Gin" became the name for the gin produced near that city. Unfortunately, gin quickly became the crack of the British Empire: it was cheap and potent, and spread to every aspect of British—and eventually American—society.

During Prohibition, a legion of aspiring Jay Gatsby types made a living by mixing industrial-grade alcohol with juniper oil and lemon peel in bathtubs, thus ensuring the American population a steady supply of illegal spirits. While such "bathtub gin" has taken its place in American mythology along with flapper dresses and songs like "Yes, We Have No Bananas," this tipple was vile enough to make even the hardiest swear off drinking forever. Happily, Prohibition was a passing fad, and the original London Dry grew in popularity during the next half century. By the early 1980s, gin constituted nearly 10 percent of the American liquor market.

GIMLET

For some reason, gimlets have earned a reputation as the drink of cliché for private eyes, cynical newspaper reporters, and tired middle-management types. In David Mamet's play *Glengarry Glen Ross*, for in-

stance, the victim of charismatic real estate sales-
man Richard Roma is introduced as drinking a gimlet. Yet
the gimlet has a fine prep pedigree. After all, on one account, the word *gimlet* derives from a Middle English word
for "boring tool," the device that was used to drill holes in
kegs of lime juice sent with British sailors on long voyages.
According to another story, it was the invention of Sir T. O.
Gimlette, a surgeon and officer of the Royal Navy. Either
way, the gimlet has enduring roots in the Anglo sailing tradition: it not only prevents scurvy, but it hits the spot after a
rigorous day on the yacht.

> **2 OZ. GIN**
>
> **½ OZ. LIME JUICE**

**Shake the gin and lime juice with ice. Strain into a
cocktail glass.**

ACCESSORY: *Lilly Pulitzer*
ACTIVITY: *Lunching*
DON'T: *Drink on an empty stomach*

NOTE: **Real preps eschew vodka gimlets.**

GIN AND TONIC

Given American prepdom's Anglophiliac tendencies
and taste for dryness (see chapter 7, "At the Club"),
it's inevitable that London Dry gin would burrow its
way into the prep universe. Mix it with tonic water,
and you get the favored weapon in the prep drink arsenal,
the fabled gin and tonic, or as it's more popularly known,

the G&T. When mixed well, and sipped on the back deck of a Sag Harbor beach house at 7:32 p.m. on a Friday, there's really nothing better. Such sublimity doesn't come without practice, however. When mixed badly, usually by a young and inexperienced barkeeper, the G&T is a frightening concoction that assaults the innocent like polyester double-knit. The mis-mixing malefactor invariably deduces that since the drink's called a gin and tonic, not a tonic and gin, gin must thereby constitute some large portion of the drink. When confronted with such disasters, the prep will either pour the mess into the sand, or discreetly add enough tonic to restore balance. The moral is clear: As with much else in prep life, including summering, excellence in mixing the G&T is all about submitting yourself to a tradition that's bigger and older than you are, and living by a rule of due proportion.

2 OZ. GIN

TONIC WATER

Pour gin into Collins glass over ice. Add tonic water to fill and stir. Garnish with a lime wedge.

ACCESSORY: *Whites*

ACTIVITY: *Tennis*

DON'T: *Drink before Memorial Day or after Labor Day*

RUM RUNNER

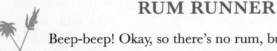

Beep-beep! Okay, so there's no rum, but the lime and pineapple keep it tropical; the gin and bitters keep it WASPy.

1½ OZ. GIN

1 OZ. PINEAPPLE JUICE

¾ OZ. LIME JUICE

1 TSP. SUGAR

1 DASH BITTERS

Shake with ice and strain over ice cubes into old-fashioned glass rimmed with salt.

ACCESSORY: *Sperry Top-Siders*

ACTIVITY: *Sneaking friends into the drive-in in the family Land Rover*

DON'T: *Earn yourself this nickname*

TOM COLLINS

Mr. Collins has sustained a bit of controversy in preppy circles through the decades. Some find him too much like a bad neighbor in some suburban cul-de-sac: sweet and cloying on the surface, essentially sour underneath, inevitably vulgar. We disagree. Some of the Tom Collins mixes out there are a little tart, but with a few friends on a hot Connecticut afternoon, Mr. Collins can be sociable and witty, and fine company.

The Tom Collins first made his appearance on the drink scene sometime in the early 1900s. No one really knows his origin: one story has it that the drink was named after an apocryphal New Jersey bartender; yet another holds that it derives from an older drink named John Collins, which was popular during the Civil War. There's no drink on record called a Phil Collins, however, despite Patrick Bateman's long-winded discourses on his music in

WHO'S PREPPIER—MICHAEL MYERS OR JASON VOORHEES?

It was tough being a summer camp counselor in the 1980s. If suffering from hangovers in uncomfortable top bunks wasn't bad enough, one had the added worry that an ax-wielding maniac would show up to make one's headache worse. The "mad slasher" horror film subgenre sparked by *Halloween* (1978) and *Friday the 13th* (1980) struck many as tasteless—hardly preppy at all. Yet, one may wonder, was madras secretly bleeding underneath?

MICHAEL MYERS FROM *HALLOWEEN* SERIES

ANTAGONISTS: *Halloween* heroine Laurie Strode played by Jamie Lee Curtis (Choate, '76). Co-star P. J. Soles ("Totally!") attended schools throughout Europe, South America, and Africa and eventually graduated from now-defunct New York women's college Briarcliff. *Preppy.*

SETTING: Suburban Illinois public school and tree-lined street during Halloween. *If New Trier, Highland Park, or Lake Forest, perhaps preppy.*

SIGNATURE LOOK: Specially modified William Shatner "Captain Kirk" mask. *Not preppy.*

JASON VOORHEES FROM *FRIDAY THE 13TH* SERIES

ANTAGONISTS: **Camp counselors who drink beer and play strip Monopoly. ("I'll be the boot.") Actors in** *Friday the 13th* **include Mark Nelson (Princeton '78) and Harry Lillis Crosby III—Bing's son—who nowadays works as a managing director at Merrill Lynch.** *Friday the 13th Part 2* **(1981) heroine Ginny played by Amy Steel, who attended the Kent School during the mid-1970s.** *Preppy.*

SETTING: **Camp Crystal Lake (a.k.a. "Camp Blood").** *Friday the 13th* **filmed at Camp No-Be-Bo-Sco in Blairstown, New Jersey;** *Friday the 13th Part 2* **filmed in Kent, Connecticut.** *Friday the 13th* **script written by Victor Miller (Milton Academy '58, Yale '62). Miller taught at the Hill School, Pottstown, Pennsylvania, from 1963 to 1966. In a later** *Fangoria* **interview, Miller said, "The camp I always thought was in someplace like New Hampshire or Vermont, one of those exclusive places most kids don't get to go to."** *Preppy.*

SIGNATURE LOOK: **Hockey mask.** *Obviously preppy.*

CONCLUSION: **In this battle royale, Jason wins. As did all preps who snuck flasks into the last remaining drive-in theaters.**

Bret Easton Ellis's novel *American Psycho*. Then again, Bateman was more yup than prep.

> 2 OZ. GIN
> 1 OZ. LEMON JUICE
> 1 TBS. SUGAR
> CLUB SODA OR SELTZER

Add ice cubes to the eponymous glass and pour in the gin. Add the lemon juice, sugar, and club soda to fill. Stir and serve with a wedge of lemon.

ACCESSORY: *Seersucker*
ACTIVITY: *Happy hour*
DON'T: *Order in a jokey way*

Renters: Vodka Drinks

HYANNISPORT HAPPY HOUR

Summer is sweet for those lucky enough to spend it on old Cape Cod. Few are able to sneak a peek at the Kennedy Compound, but on rainy days there's always the free Ocean Spray factory tour. They don't call it Cranberry Cocktail for nothing.

CAPE CODDER (JACKIE)

Known as the "Rangoon Ruby" during the post–World War II Polynesian Trader Vic's craze, it was renamed the "Bog Fog" in the 1960s. Luckily for us, the name was changed yet again. In fact, half the pleasure of this drink is in the ordering. A favorite of Seven

Sisters students, as much for the health benefits of the cranberry juice as for the alcohol.

> 1 1/2 OZ. VODKA
> CRANBERRY JUICE

Pour vodka into Collins glass over ice. Add cranberry juice to fill. Stir well. Garnish with a wedge of lime.

ACCESSORY: *Sunglasses (you know what kind)*
ACTIVITY: *Silent auction*
DON'T: *Spill on your white dungarees*

MADRAS (ETHEL)

Drink as you dress!

> 1 1/2 OZ. VODKA
> 4 OZ. CRANBERRY JUICE
> 1 OZ. ORANGE JUICE

Pour into Collins glass over ice. Garnish with a wedge of lime.

ACCESSORY: *Mad about plaid*
ACTIVITY: *Touch football*
DON'T: *Stir if you want to maintain the "madras" effect*

SEABREEZE (JOAN)

Ah—the salt air, the outside shower, the full-bellied clams, the horseshoes in the backyard, the jigsaw puzzle for rainy days, the faded paperbacks, the shell art, the flip-flops, the breeze rustling the screen door.

> 1½ OZ. VODKA
> 4 OZ. CRANBERRY JUICE
> 1 OZ. GRAPEFRUIT JUICE

Pour into Collins glass over ice. Garnish with a wedge of lime.

ACCESSORY: *Windbreaker*
ACTIVITY: *Mini-golf*
DON'T: *Come in without washing the sand off your feet*

KAMIKAZE

The thing that most urban dwellers have to adjust to most when summering, besides the quiet, is the dark. There are places in Manhattan where you can read walking down the street at night. When you're driving alone at night in Chilmark, there are no lights. The dark closes up behind you as soon as your high beams cut through it. It's like waking up out of a deep sleep and feeling your way to the bathroom. And not only are there no streetlights, there are no street signs either. And in the fog? Forget it. Who knows when a deer will jump into your wind-

shield? When a skunk will zap you with "the juice"? Mos-
quitos? Tics? Is it time to go back to the city yet?

Keep off the road. Drink a kamikaze instead.

1 OZ. VODKA

1 OZ. TRIPLE SEC

1 OZ. LIME JUICE

**Shake with ice and strain over ice cubes into old-
fashioned glass. Or for a shot, serve straight up.**

ACCESSORY: *Flashlight*
ACTIVITY: *M-80s on July 3rd*
DON'T: *Drink and drive*

VODKA TONIC

*Alice looked at Des, trying to decipher this. "You mean it's a
complete cliché? 'All recent women college graduates drink
vodka-tonics,' or something like that?"*
"Well," Des said. "Maybe."

—THE LAST DAYS OF DISCO, WITH COCKTAILS AT
PETROSSIAN AFTERWARDS BY WHIT STILLMAN

While we don't dispute the above, we chose to put
vodka tonics in the summering chapter rather than
the debutante chapter. There is a reason why grand-
mothers and aunts and yes, recent women college
graduates, drink vodka tonics. In fact, it's the most com-
monly ordered vodka drink in the land. The tonic sweetens
the drink, so that you can hardly taste the vodka. And

there's no fruit juice to add on the pounds. Of course, it's a unisex drink, but we especially admire those women who order it. It's full of booze, dammit.

2 OZ. VODKA

TONIC WATER

Pour vodka into Collins glass over ice. Add tonic water to fill and stir. Garnish with a lime wedge.

ACCESSORY: *Linen*
ACTIVITY: *Bridge*
DON'T: *Use the "and"*

Year-Rounders: Rum Drinks
CUBA LIBRE

Originally made with gin and bitters, the cuba libre of the '80s was basically a rum and coke but with lime juice. If you are going to order it, pronounce it correctly: KOO-buh LEE-bray. It's the only way to drink Coke if you're a prep.

2 OZ. LIGHT RUM

1 TBSP. LIME JUICE

COLA

Fill Collins glass with ice cubes, rum, lime juice, and twist of lime. Add cola to fill.

ACCESSORY: *Cigar*
ACTIVITY: *Whiffle ball*
DON'T: *Get bogged down in the politics*

PLANTERS PUNCH

Jamaican sugar planters enjoyed the punch, thus the name. Enjoy it at engagement lawn parties under tents in Connecticut.

> 2 OZ. RUM
>
> 2 OZ. ORANGE JUICE
>
> 2 OZ. PINEAPPLE JUICE
>
> 1 OZ. MYERS'S RUM (JAMAICAN)
>
> 1 OZ. LIME JUICE
>
> 1 TSP. SUGAR

Shake and strain into a Collins glass over fresh ice, and fill with soda water. Garnish with orange slice and cherry.

ACCESSORY: *Your friend's fiancée's great-aunt*
ACTIVITY: *Swatting away bugs*
DON'T: *Worry—it's really a cocktail, not a punch*

RUM AND TONIC

The silent member of the tonic triumvirate, the rum and tonic is the drink of choice for the mid-August going-away beachside soiree. The summer's coming to an end soon, the Salinger and Steinbeck still sit in a pile on the floor of your room, and your crush is still unrecipro-cated. Enjoy the sunset.

> 2 OZ. RUM
>
> TONIC WATER

**Pour rum into Collins glass over ice. Add tonic water
to fill and stir. Garnish with a lime wedge.**

ACCESSORY: *Daddy's college sweatshirt*
ACTIVITY: *Backgammon*
DON'T: *Step in the poison ivy*

The Uninvited Guest
LONG ISLAND ICED TEA

Plain old genteel iced tea doesn't quite cut it for New
York summers. New Yorkers, especially those sleeping
on the floor next to fifty strangers in a Hamptons
summer share, need something a little, um, stronger.
It's what you make on Saturday with the leftover booze
from Friday. (Let's hope you have enough booze left over.)

> ½ SHOT VODKA
>
> ½ SHOT TEQUILA
>
> ½ SHOT GIN
>
> ½ SHOT LIGHT RUM
>
> ½ SHOT TRIPLE SEC
>
> 1 TBSP. OF LEMON JUICE
>
> COLA

**Combine all ingredients and pour over ice in Collins
glass. Add cola for color. Garnish with a wedge of
lemon.**

ACCESSORY: *Cucumber sandwiches*
ACTIVITY: *Party-hopping*
DON'T: *Have more than two*

The Wall of Shame

WATCH OUT FOR CRABS: SEX ON THE BEACH

Reagan-era repression yields the summer's most infamous sex-themed drink.

THREE

Do Brahmins Drink Budweiser?: Yes, But They Own Better Horses

"Beer, once the drink of the working class, is now making its appearance in white-wine and Champagne circles and is said to be the beverage of the eighties. Are we ever glad!"

—JULEE ROSSO AND SHEILA LUKINS,
   THE SILVER PALATE COOKBOOK (1982)

The *Mayflower* brought forth unto New England more than just those families whose names would fill private school alumni rosters and *The Social Register* for the next several hundred years. As Pilgrim William Bradford would explain in his journal, his group had some quite practical reasons for landing in Plymouth, Massachusetts: "We could not now take time for further search or consideration, our victuals being much spent, especially our Beere." The descendants of Bradford and the other Pilgrims inherited not only their ancestors' love of boating while drinking, they continued to celebrate the virtues of a keg.

One might think that no matter how entrenched in tradition beer was, preps would have moved onto something else once beer started cavorting with blue jeans, baseball, and hot dogs on the populist hit parade. But preppy drinking is about paradoxes. One must always allow for the possibility that something else was brewing beneath the surface.

For preppies, beer drinking has a dual function. Beer's "common man" aura nicely camouflages one's assets. (Prep youth are taught never to flaunt their wealth, education, or background.) And while the fine wine or spiffy highball—perhaps along with a gift subscription to *The New Yorker*—are the sure signs of established adulthood, beer drinking is linked inextricably to good times at one's alma mater. Prep school and college are considered the best eight—or more—years of a prep's life. It may be bad form to publicize

one's CV, but the prep *is* expected to use one's prep school
and undergraduate experience to network for jobs and sexual partners. It is while preparing, after all, that one learned
how to party *en masse*, cementing lifelong friendships and
memories. In those raging parties in the woods behind the
golf course, however, there was not always time nor space
for a good bartender to do things right. In the name of simplicity and efficiency, virtues both highly valued by preps,
such events actually required beer—and lots of it. Thus, the
taste of beer is always associated with the bloom of youth
and a prep's first buzz—two things they will spend the rest
of their adulthood trying to recapture.

Beer Snob?

But not just any beer! In some sense, most beers taste pretty
much the same. Yet while university students have been
beer guzzlers since the glory days of the Universities of
Padua and Paris in the late Middle Ages, *preppy* beer drink-

BOTTLE OF BEER

"I'm proud of my trophies/like my empty beer cans/stacked in rows up the wall/To impress all my friends," once sang The Dead Kennedys in their song "Terminal Preppie." Sorry Jello Biafra, but as even Sidney Poitier, Jr., could tell you, preps drink their beer in bottles. In John Guare's play *Six Degrees of Separation* (1990), based on a real incident from 1982, Trent Conway, a closeted gay Manhattan prep attending M.I.T. plays Professor Henry Higgins to a young black street hustler. "And you," Trent says, "you say 'boddle'—'I'll have a boddle of beer. It's *bottle*. Say *bottle* of beer." While no one confuses M.I.T. with its preppy Cambridge neighbor, Mr. Conway's diction and knowledge of preppy drinking habits gives away

ing in 1980s Charlottesville and Newport had a character all its own. So what were the great preppy beers of the 1980s? It depends on whom you ask. Someone who was not there at the time will answer with some domestic microbrew. Someone who *was* there may answer with some obscure Czech brew. Both would be wrong.

One must reiterate: *Preppy beer is not necessarily yuppie beer.* The *yuppie* of the mid to late '80s drank all sorts of trendy exotic beers—from anything dark with a hard-to-pronounce German name to anything produced by Trappist monks. The confusion is understandable. The thinking his prep rearing. For while smashing a beer *can* against one's head does offer a certain swaggering pleasure, it is a pastime best suited for metalheads. The only exceptions to the bottle rule are keg parties, where custom requires the use of disposable plastic cups (although the well-prepared prep will bring his own prep school athletic award stein); or bars, where iced pilsner or pint glasses are *de rigueur* for draft beer. How much discernment can you expect from somebody named "Jello" anyway?

NOTE: Although beer purists prefer brown bottles, which block out the bright light that can affect the beer and give it a "skunky" taste, green bottles have been around longer and thus tend to be somewhat preppier.

seems to be that the more undrinkable or obscure a beer is, the more "pure" or "real" it is. Thus, imports such as Chimay and indie beers like Harpoon are oft thought "preppy" in virtue of their "tony" European lineage or microbrew "cache." This is a real misconception.

Unlike the fast-track B-schoolers and Ferrari aficionados of the time, preppies didn't particularly worry about brand names *qua* brand names: it wasn't about proving anything. Secure in their way of life and "status," they were free to enjoy the simple pleasures available in any well-stocked backyard cooler. Of course, to enjoy the "smooth-drinking" beer was, and is, at least to flirt with vulgarity. In a 1982 *Time* magazine report, beer industry consultant Leo Bernstein explained the matter in these terms: "Lighter beer was a marketing decision when American brewers wanted to enlarge the market by making a beer you could drink a lot of. With German beers, you can't drink so much or the bitterness will make your mouth go numb." But for preps—who *enjoyed* getting sloshed—the flirtation was worth it: after all, the demands of "purity" never prevented the average prep from owning a small library of Monarch notes. While preppy beer drinkers had their preferences—some certainly better than others by any standard—classic preppy beer drinking ultimately wouldn't worry about keeping up with the Joneses or the Higginbothams; it wouldn't enroll in "beer-of-the-month" clubs or attempt home-brewing; rather, it would lift its bottle with the confidence of tradition and say, "Cheers."

So bring along your key chain bottle openers—and don't fill up too quickly.

The Top 18 Preppy Beers of the 1980s (In Descending Order)

18. MILWAUKEE'S BEST

"The Beast"

THEN: Although the mark of the beast in this case is just a prominent Miller insignia, Milwaukee's Best is that brewery's off-brand, the down-market Chaps to their High Life Polo. This foamy not-so-specialty is what you'd drink when it was homecoming weekend, and you and your friends were heading out to get some beer for the game, but one of you decided to pull a "neutral drop" in your parents' Saab, but in so doing, caused the transmission to clunk to the pavement with a sad cloud of smoke, and since you'd owe your parents quite a bit of money to repair the damages, you'd all be looking for something cheap by which to do penance. Milwaukee's Best was your beer.

NOW: Still on the loose

WHO: Marty McFly wannabes

WHERE: In denial

17. BUSCH

"Head for the Mountains—Please"

THEN: Some people equate this with its fun-loving cousin, Budweiser, but this really *is* tasteless—a case where "smooth, refreshing" taste is just a euphemism for "Perrier-manqué." (See Chapter 9, "Taking the Waters.") It's a mystery: Preps who can buy far better kegs at roughly the same price continue to pick this beer for lawn parties year after year, despite its aggressive tastelessness. Perhaps misguided nostalgia's at work: For preps coming of age in the 1980s in parts of the country with tough carding laws, this was the beer that puckish older friends would buy for their underage fellows and siblings on Friday nights. Perhaps, then, the continued success of Busch is some cosmic joke. No matter the explanation, Busch is the beer you buy when the party is going to be big and undiscerning.

NOW: Still the undisputed King of Keg Fodder

WHO: The innocent and young

WHERE: The fetid dorm basement of youth, with "Louie, Louie" as musical accompaniment

ROLL OUT THE BARRELS: KEGGING KEPT DIGNIFIED

Despite its thuggish reputation, the beer keg is not only for "Chug!"-chanting cretins in baseball caps. Preppy kegging style aims to be well mannered. One fills one's friends' cups before one refills one's own. Preps hold their cups close to their bodies, mid-chest, rather like cocktails. And they don't spill beer on others—at least not before 2 A.M.

When preppy New England college towns *en masse* enacted silly keg license requirements throughout the 1990s, licentious preps switched over to the keg's newfangled little brother, the party ball. While these contraptions cut down on the bureaucracy, the real prep, as always, will keep things classic. When one considers that a properly cleaned and maintained keg container can stay usable for years—some kegs out there are upwards of two *decades* old—the historical value of the keg makes it too good to pass up—that, and the sheer efficiency of it all.

16. GROLSCH PREMIUM LAGER

"The Other Dutch Beer"

THEN: While the spiffy swing-top caps and green embossed bottles gave this import some undeniable prep cred, fancy caps and embossing do not a drinkable beer make. To be sure, this nasty, hoppy lager is perhaps the most over-

But before you can kill a keg, you have to know how to tap it.

- First, you'll need a keg tap. Since there are five different taps in use for the different beers of the world, you'll need the tap that your beer requires. Happily, most American beers use the same model, so if you own it, you're in luck. Otherwise, when you buy your keg, you can rent it. The clerk at the liquor store or beer distributor will set you up.

- Once you've found the right tap and have lugged home your keg, let it settle for an hour or two.

- It's tap time. Remove the dust cover from your keg. Make sure that both the keg's beer faucet and your tap are in the "off" position. Align the lug locks on the tavern head of your tap with the lug housing in the top of the keg and insert the tavern head.

- Rotate the on/off valve one-quarter turn clockwise. Your keg is now tapped; let the party begin.

rated beer in the prep pantheon. Like its very name, Grolsch is harsh, turgid, and heavy, and the pains required to drink it prove punishment enough for any preppy who may be tempted by the clever packaging.

NOW: Still fooling them

WHO: A cappella singers

15. RED STRIPE

"Jammin' "

THEN: This Jamaican lager is best enjoyed from the trunk of a fake wood–paneled Country Squire station wagon in the parking lot outside a Ziggy Marley and the Melody Makers concert. By common consent, the hops nicely balance out the odor of patchouli, among other things.

NOW: Same, except for the car

WHO: Trustifarians

WHERE: Mixmaster Tom Cruise orders some for the ladies at a Jamaican resort in *Cocktail*

14. FOSTER'S

"Who Can It Be Now?"

THEN: While preps tend not to be so saucy for matters Aussie (they hail Britannia, not the Commonwealth), the hulking "oil can" made this brew stand out on the shelves— when it didn't make them cave in. How did you actually hold one?

NOW: Marketed as "Australian for Beer" by Melbourne's Carlton and United Brewing Company, it's actually brewed in Canada. A dash yuppie, but those cans still come mighty big . . .

WHO: Guys who rowed crew . . . for one week

WHERE: Friday nights in Charlottesville, bemoaning the Japanese trade deficit while watching *Mad Max* on its first cable run

"The Mile-High Beer"

THEN: Coors was once a local item, a regional beer produced in a humble brewery in Golden, Colorado. During the early 1970s, however, the company's beer became a big hit among the preppy skier contingent, who snuck the brew across state lines in their Volkswagens and Peugeots; by the mid-1970s, the beer was the fourth bestselling brand in the United States. Plus, it had cool push tabs that you couldn't find on any other beer. Yet a bitter 1977 strike led to a union boycott of Coors products, and during the 1980s, the allegedly hard-right political predilections of company management earned Coors a reputation for crypto-fascism among socially conscious preps. That Coors was one of Henry Kissinger's favorite beers didn't help; nor did the company's founding grant for the Heritage Foundation; still less did the company's introduction of Zima in '92.

NOW: Coors Light served on tap at the Princeton Club of New York

WHO: The CB ski-jacket contingent

WHERE: Vail

---

12 . BUDWEISER

"The King"

THEN: At first blush, one might expect *the* standard American pilsner to be too mass-crass to find a place on this list. To some extent, this suspicion is correct—no prep worth his salt would have anything to do with the rat-like "Spuds McKenzie"—but on a hot day, it would be misguided snobbery to overlook the simple pleasures of an iced pilsner glass filled with Bud. It would also overlook the deeper fact that more than a few prep kegs and mini-refrigerators were filled with the King of Beers; visit any Ivy League dormitory to this day, and you *will* find Budweiser posters on students' walls. While Bud is mass marketed, so is the Volvo; and like that car, Bud provides moderation, durability, and safety—key excellences in the preppy catalogue of virtues. Long live the Clydesdales.

NOW: Still king

WHO: Bookish preps aspiring to "regular guy" status; rugby players with broken noses

WHERE: Best enjoyed from a cooler during summer barbecues at the country house in Connecticut

11. CORONA

"La Cerveza Mas Fina"

THEN: Corona has an admittedly divided audience. Old school Dos Equis fans find it overpriced, over-marketed swill; others defend its special charms on a hot summer day. All agree, though, that you have to drink it with a lime wedge. While Spanish class was second-sailing for those who couldn't get the nasals down in French, and while the California ideology of the 1980s may have made all things sunny a national pastime, the taste for Corona actually had a respectable prep pedigree. While putting in the lime might seem a little affected, Corona was a decent beer for housewarming parties of friends who'd just moved to the Upper East Side. Like hand-woven friendship bracelets and Guatemalan pullovers, Corona was a fine addition to 1980s preppy life.

NIP AT NITE: HI, BOB

It's fitting, somehow, that the understated Bob Newhart would inspire *the* preppy drinking game. The characters on Bob's 1970s sitcom *The Bob Newhart Show* greet Bob, the show's main character, a grand total of 256 times during the course of the 142 episodes series. We don't know who first noticed this—or why—but apparently it was enough for someone and "Hi, Bob," the drinking game was born. It doesn't take much. And now you can play, too.

1 television

1 VCR (*The Bob Newhart Show* is available on VHS—let's hope a DVD is forthcoming.)

1 drink (They don't actually say "Hi" that often.)

Friends (The number is your call. Or, the beauty of this game is you can play alone!)

Whenever anyone says "Hi, Bob!" repeat "Hi, Bob!" and take a drink.

NOTES: Episode 49 ("Big Brother is Watching") contains the most "Hi, Bobs"—seven. You can substitute episodes of *Newhart* and drink to "Hi, Dick!" but it's not quite as satisfying.

NOW: The bestselling American import, now beating Heineken

WHO: G.D.P.s—Grateful Dead preps—that 1980s subculture known for their scruffy WASP looks, dancing bear bumper stickers, and pre–Jennifer Garner Denison degrees

WHERE: VW buses

---

10. ST. PAULI GIRL

"Full-Bodied"

THEN: Along with Beck's and Löwenbräu, the third member of the preppy German lager trio. First available nationally in the U.S. in 1975, the asyntactic name of this brew from Bremen gave it a certain old world charm, as did the eponymous beer-hall waitress on the label.

NOW: The overlooked stepdaughter of the classic German imports, S.P.G. got lost in the crowd during the '80s. But like the Beetle, she's back.

WHO: Good ol' boys.

WHERE: Birdwatching.

---

9. KNICKERBOCKER

"The Headless Horseman"

THEN: Originally brewed by Col. Jacob Ruppert, owner of the Yankees, this was taken over by Stroh's/Heileman Brewing Company. Cases of Knickerbocker were always a little beaten looking, and you couldn't help wondering where the bottles had been, but one has to love a beer whose mascot in its glory days was Washington Irving. ("They who drink beer will think beer," once wrote Mr. Irving himself.) A slightly more refined Pabst Blue Ribbon for the Eastern Establishment, Knickerbocker was best served very cold to the very drunk.

NOW: Went out of business at the end of 1997

WHO: Twelve College exchange students

WHERE: Dartmouth Winter Carnival

8. ROLLING ROCK

"33"

THEN: The prize beer of the Tito brothers—Frank, Joseph, Robert, Ralph, and Anthony (no mention of Jermaine or Marlon)—this extra pale ale was first brewed in 1939 in Latrobe, Pennsylvania, birthplace of Mr. Rogers. Another case of a regional beer that took off nationally, Rolling Rock is smooth drinking, though with peculiar green olive overtones.

NOW: It's everywhere

WHO: The favorite beer of *The Last Days of Disco*'s Jimmy Steinway

WHERE: When you're going to a party at a yuppie's house but don't want to spend a lot of money, and know that Bud would be ill-received

7. ANCHOR STEAM

"The Bay Brew"

THEN: Made in San Francisco since 1896, Anchor Steam earned its reputation from locals. Through the 1960s, saloons around San Francisco served this up to a burgeoning Beatnik population who enjoyed the beer's cheap price and rich flavor. When the struggling Market Street brewery eventually filed for bankruptcy, however,

"33" BOTTLES OF BEER
ON THE WALL

Along with "Just what does the Skull and Bones tomb look like inside?" few topics have elicited such wide-ranging preppy speculation as the meaning of the mysterious "33" on Rolling Rock bottles. Does it have something to do with the end of Prohibition? With the re-founding of Latrobe Brewing Company? (Latrobe Brewing Company was founded in 1893, shut down during Prohibition, and reopened in 1933.) Is it just a lucky number? Or does it somehow contain a secret backward message?

Actually, none of the above. According to author Cecil Adams, who interviewed Frank Tito, the number was a "colossal accident." As it turns out, the Bros. Tito could not decide upon a slogan. Some favored something short and zippy; others favored a treatise on beer-making. Eventually, somebody came up with the slogan that still appears on the bottle: "Rolling Rock from glass-lined tanks in the Laurel Highlands. We tender this premium beer for your enjoyment as a tribute to your good taste. It comes from the mountain springs to you." It clocked in at a moderate 33 words, and the author wrote a "33" next to it. The Bros. went for it.

When the first bottles came back from the factory, the Bros. were horrified to discover that not only the slogan, but the "33" as well, made it onto the beer. Given the dire U.S. economy of the time, the Titos had no choice but to accept the bottles. The number has remained ever since.

Fritz Maytag, the twenty-six-year-old heir to the washing machine dynasty and a Stanford philosophy major, came to the rescue. Although preps usually avoid philosophy in favor of English, government, or history, Maytag's analytical skills paid off: after buying the brewery, he turned it around, and established an early microbrew standard for adventurous Bay Area preppy beer drinkers of the late '70s. Amber-colored, full-bodied, and hoppy, Anchor Steam was available in nineteen states, including Massachusetts, by 1982.

NOW: Enjoyed by beer snobs

WHO: Junior members of the Bohemian Club

WHERE: Ultimate Frisbee in Golden Gate Park

6. AMSTEL LIGHT

"The Chick Beer"

THEN: At the height of 1980s Heineken-mania, the Dutch brewer wanted to get in on the light beer explosion taking over America. The thing was, Heineken already was pretty light, so realizing that they'd bought the name "Amstel" from another brewery in the late 1960s, Heineken unleashed Amstel Light on America as their 1980s light beer.

NOW: Today's bestselling light import. Served on tap at the Yale Club of New York

WHO: The Farmington and Nightingale-Bamford set

WHERE: Art gallery openings and book parties

5. LABATT'S BLUE

"Big Blue"

THEN: While some Canadians tend to be too wonky, technocratic, and/or French to sustain true wooden-mallard preppy traditionalism (see chapter 8, "The Wrath of Grapes"), they nevertheless do know how to make preppy beer. John Kinder Labatt founded his brewery in 1847, and his Canadian pilsner made preps happy all through the Trudeau and Mulroney years. Labatt's Blue was originally known as Labatt's Pilsner, but given the beer's blue labels and the brewery's support of the Winnipeg Canadian Football League team, the Blue Bombers, the beer ended up with its new appellation. As one might expect from the brewers of the Canadian versions of Budweiser and Bud Light, Labatt's is pretty smooth. It was also the first Canadian beer to come with a twist-off cap (in 1984).

NOW: The #1 bestselling beer in Canada and the #3 import in the United States

WHO: Former Coors drinkers

WHERE: Reportedly quite popular at Vassar during the early coed years

---

4. BECK'S

"The Keymaster"

THEN: The taste is like honey that tapers off into a kind of bitterness. Although German, it has nothing in common with, say, Werner Herzog: it's mellow, it stays within budget, and you probably wouldn't find it lugging a riverboat over a mountain. In the 1990s, this would earn a reputation for being a yuppie beer, but that's not really its fault. Like Löwenbräu (see page 62), this lager is brewed according to the "Reinheistgebot"—i.e., the German purity law of 1516. Preps wonder what the skeleton key on its label is supposed to unlock. (The city gates of Bremen, Germany, of course.)

NOW: Served on tap at the Harvard Club of New York

WHO: Preppy law students

WHERE: The Rathskellar

---

3. MOLSON GOLDEN

"MG"

THEN: Founded in 1786 by John Molson, Molson is the oldest brewery in North America. MG is a malty blend of ale and lager—another fine brew from the land of the maple leaf. With approximately one-quarter of the U.S. import market under its control during the early '80s, Molson was Heineken's biggest competitor during the era's preppy beer-drinking showdown.

NOW: Molson is still brewed in Montreal, right up the river from Canton, New York, home of St. Lawrence University

WHO: St. Lawrence University hockey player preps. It was their safety school

WHERE: In a Stowe ski lodge while you wear a down-filled vest

> *"[S]kiing is the ideal sport for Putney as one may ski chiefly to enjoy himself, the air, the snow."*
> —THE PUTNEY SCHOOL, PUTNEY, VERMONT

2 . LÖWENBRAÜ

"The Lion's Brew"

THEN: The ad campaign that J. Walter Thompson ran for Löwenbraü in its late-1970s and early-1980s heyday nicely encapsulates the prep beer-drinking ethos in all its simplicity: "Here's to good friends," sang the deep-throated Arthur Prysock. "Tonight is kinda special." While preps have focused their attention elsewhere over the last decade or so, Löwenbraü entered the 1980s neck-in-neck with Heineken as the leading imported beer. In fact, in 1977, Löwenbraü *was* the leading import. Brewed in Munich according to the "Reinheitsgabot," this lager presents a healthy mean between traditional *echt*-German beers and, say, Busch. However, in the late-1970s, Löwenbraü entered into an agreement with Miller, according to which the American brewer would produce the beer domestically; the agreement went according to plan, except in the 1980s, Miller "reformulated" the beer with one of their old beer recipes to compete with domestic brews.

NOW: By the late 1990s, the German company was no longer amused by Miller's bastardization and willingness to let this one flounder in a competitive market. Once the Miller contract expired in October 1999, Löwenbraü struck up an agreement with Labatt's to import the beer straight from Germany for stateside distribution. Although Löwenbraü now sells the beer with a dippy advertising campaign aimed at craven *Maxim* readers with hankerings for Teutonic beer hall waitresses, the beer seems primed to make a comeback.

WHO: Anti-Heineken holdouts

WHERE: Eagle-eyed viewers will catch a few glimpses of it in *St. Elmo's Fire*

1. HEINEKEN

"Greenie"

THEN: Founded by Gerard Adriaan Heineken, this lager was first brewed in 1873, and first showed up in the United States in the 1880s. The first post-Prohibition import as well, Heineken is a beer from the continent for the continent beer drinker: it's light, peppy, smooth, and rounded out with a distinct fruitiness. Go to Amsterdam for a bachelor party of the damned and you'll see Heineken logos all over the place. The beer comes in light and dark versions, but the light version's green bottle earned the beer its famous nickname, "Greenie." (Preps usually avoided the other nickname, "Heinie.") In the early '80s, Heineken constituted approximately 98 percent of all beer exported from the Netherlands; in the United States, the beer controlled an astonishing 40 percent of the import market. Although eventually hijacked by Gordon Gekko–types, Heineken is preppy at heart. Its moment of mid-'80s celluloid glory came in *Blue Velvet*, wherein gas-addled Dennis Hopper asks poor Kyle MacLachlan what kind of beer he drinks. "Heineken," MacLachlan mumbles. "Heineken?" grunts Hopper. "Pabst's Blue Ribbon!" It was just the kind of response anyone might expect from the director of *Easy Rider*. As the preppy Virginian with sexual problems on *Sex and the City*, MacLachlan seems fated to play a put-upon Heineken drinker, no matter what the decade.

NOW: Served on tap at the Yale Club of New York
WHO: Who didn't?
WHERE: Every benefit fund-raiser from 1980 to the present day

The Wall of Shame

LESS WASTED, MORE FILLING: THE NONALCOHOLIC BEER THING

O'Doul's. Sharp's. Buckler. It was a nice idea, but face it: for preps, beer without the alcohol was like a Weejun without the penny.

FOUR

Come Out Swinging:
Drinks for Debs

"Edith had danced herself into that tired, dreamy state habitual only with debutantes, a state equivalent to the glow of a noble soul after several long highballs. Her mind floated vaguely on the bosom of the music; her partners changed with the unreality of phantoms under the colorful shifting dusk, and to her present coma it seemed as if days had passed since the dance began. She had talked on many fragmentary subjects with many men. She had been kissed once and made love to six times."

—F. Scott Fitzgerald, "May Day"

No, we're not talking about what some college kids do during their first Thanksgiving home from school. Nor are we referring to the Diana Ross song. Rather, in the 1980s, certain families revived the archaic practice of formally introducing their daughters into society. In greater Dallas, it was time to throw a beauty pageant; in the establishment East, it was debutante season—an excuse to throw a bigger party than anyone else.

Not all preps are debs; not all debs are preps. The daughter of the Sarasota podiatrist may make her debut in white satin, but never live a page of Salinger; conversely, the Bowdoin tennis player born to the owners of the humble Maine antique store will never shop for a gaudy display of pearls. But some overlap was inevitable. In a 1984 piece for *The New York Times Magazine*, D. Susan Barron described a girl's debut as "a celebration of wealth, a familial rite and an affirmation of social identity." Indeed, after the social upheavals and questionable fashion trends of the '60s and '70s, the debutante ball of the '80s represented a return to simpler, more stable times. Those prep daughters who did come out—typically around age eighteen or nineteen, at elaborate balls held during the winter months—were continuing a tradition begun stateside in Philadelphia in 1748. (As with most prep culture, the debutante tradition found its roots in the Old Country—i.e., England.) While initiated as a way for Mummy and Daddy to present their daughters to socially registered suitors, the deb ball gradually evolved—or devolved, depending on your perspective—into a quaint ritual seasoned with equal dashes conspicuous philanthropy and social insecurity. Mother and daughter prepare for years for the event: the right white dress must be purchased, a saber-wielding escort or two from the local military academy lined up, the St. James Bow perfected. Falling on one's face during the bow could literally ruin a girl's life.

Despite the surface gentility of the affair, drinking plays a role before, during, and after these events. But what did these 1980s Charlottes drink? The cosmopolitan and the apple martini hadn't been invented yet, after all. And what about those debut-less girls left to fend for themselves? So-called "ladies' drinks" were appreciated by both groups. For it's a rare lady who actually *enjoys* the taste of alcohol. Women like their alcohol masked with other, sweeter tastes.

The preppy stereotypes sometimes go out the window when we're dealing with this category. Most of the following drinks are too sweet—and precious—to meet the usual stiff-upper-lip prep standards. But when it's deb night, it's your party and you can drink what you want to.

BACARDI COCKTAIL: SHIRLEY TEMPLE BLACK

Most debs have fond childhood memories of being allowed to order Shirley Temples (add grenadine to Collins glass filled with ice; top with ginger ale; decorate with orange slice and cherry). When the drink's namesake grew up, she became Nixon's ambassador to the United Nations. When her fans grew up, they replaced the ginger ale with rum.

2 OZ. BACARDI RUM

1 OZ. LIME JUICE

1 TSP. GRENADINE

Shake with ice and strain into cocktail glass

DANCE: **Samba.**

Be sure your date is not a dip.

BELLINI: PRETTY IN PINK

While known as a cocktail for ladies, that didn't stop international drinking hall-of-famer Ernest Hemingway and blithe spirit Noel Coward from enjoying this refreshing Italian aperitif back in the day—though not together. The Bellini was created in Venice in 1948 at Harry's Bar by owner Giuseppe Cipriani. Supposedly named after the Venetian painter Giovanni Bellini, it became popular on these shores when the next generation of C)prianis opened two restaurants in New York City in the mid-1980s.

> 3 OZ. PEACH NECTAR
>
> 2 DASH LEMON JUICE
>
> 1 DASH GRENADINE
>
> 3 OZ. CHAMPAGNE

Pour chilled peach nectar into champagne flute (or wineglass). Add lemon juice and grenadine. Chilled champagne to fill.

DANCE: **The fan dance.**

It's hot in Venice.

BRANDY ALEXANDER: CACAO IS FOREVER

Diamonds may be a girl's best friend, but for a deb who has spent months dieting for the big night, *chocolate* trumps all. Before the upstart chocolate martini explosion, poor little rich girls had to sneak sips from Grandmother's brandy Alexanders over the holidays. True, the drink sounds like the name of a tough, no-nonsense saloon singer, but the brandy Alexander was one of the first "girlie" drinks in town. Like said saloon singer, it's a little on the heavy side. But with its creamy chocolate overtones, it makes a good wintertime dessert pick for the deb who's heading off to Aspen post–coming out and who's left hot cocoa behind.

> 1 OZ. DARK CRÈME DE CACAO
>
> 1 OZ. BRANDY
>
> 1 OZ. HEAVY CREAM

Shake well with ice and strain into cocktail glass.

DANCE: **Burlesque.**

In private, of course.

DAIQUIRI: DOUBLE OR NOTHING

F. Scott Fitzgerald's *This Side of Paradise* (1920) features the first written reference to this citrus specialty: When not breaking the hearts of debs everywhere, self-described "romantic egotist" Amory Blaine and his Princeton posse order double daiquiris. Named after a town in Cuba near the original Bacardi rum distillery, the daiquiri was actually invented by one Jennings Cox, an American steel executive who managed offshore mines. Legend has it that he ran out of gin one night in 1896; the rest is history. The drink made its way to the mainland by way of Admiral Lucius Johnson, a Spanish-American War veteran who sampled Cox's creation and—luckily for us— imported it to Washington, D.C.'s Army Navy Club. A plaque in the club's Daiquiri Lounge immortalizes the event.

Back in Cuba, however, when *quien-es-mas-macho* Sr. Hemingway wasn't fishing for marlins or cheering at bullfights, he was ordering up custom-made sweet-'n'-bastardized versions at his favorite Havana bars. Within just decades, this version of the daiquiri was served up as fruit-freeze T.G.I.Friday's fodder.

But the deb keeps things classic. So put away the blenders and strawberries. Southern belles may be able to get away with big hair, but preppy debs don't even try.

> 1 ½ OZ. LIGHT RUM
>
> 1 OZ. LIME JUICE (FRESH, NOT ROSE'S)
>
> 1 TSP. SUGAR

Shake with ice and strain into cocktail glass.

DANCE: **Rumba.**

In the Bronx. (Whoops, we mean Riverdale.)

The Russians Are Coming: Anastasia on Ice

The debutante ball is not just for WASPs. While "preppy" may not be an international language, money certainly is. And while the competition for the most spectacular deb ball has never reached *War and Peace* proportions, a nest of young Fabergé eggs has gathered for decades to make their debuts into stateside Cyrillic society. For girls of Russian heritage, the deb circuit's all about Romanov reminiscence and the pre–Bolshevik bandstand. In fact, the mother of one of our first-year college dorm floormates used to organize one of the Russian balls. We never attended.

WHITE RUSSIAN

The coffee liqueur is helpful if you want to last until the after-party.

2 OZ. VODKA

1 OZ. COFFEE LIQUEUR

MILK OR CREAM

Pour vodka and coffee liqueur into old-fashioned glass over ice. Milk or cream to fill.

BLACK RUSSIAN

For those watching their figures.

2 OZ VODKA

1 OZ. COFFEE LIQUEUR

Pour vodka and coffee liqueur into old-fashioned glass over ice.

DANCE: **Waltz.**

Step, step, close.

SOMBRERO

Debs may not wear sombreros, but they do like their coffee-flavored brandy drinks. The sombrero got its name because the cream is supposed to float on top of the brandy like a hat. It's unclear, though, why "sombrero" was the only hat choice here. After all, the drink is not related to our southern neighbor in any way. Wouldn't top hat have been better? Or boater? Either way, consider the sombrero your white Russian substitute—Leon Trotsky style.

> 1½ OZ. COFFEE-FLAVORED BRANDY
> LIGHT CREAM

Pour brandy into old-fashioned glass over ice. Light cream to fill so that it floats on top—like a hat.

DANCE: **Cha-cha.**

Charo—everybody's favorite Love Boat *passenger!*

The Sour Sisters:
Happy Valley of the Dolls

Smith College seniors who haven't yet come out are given an opportunity on Ivy Day, held the day before graduation. The soon-to-be-graduates wear white and are given a rose to hold as they march, like virgins to a sacrifice, past a crowd of family and friends.

We don't know about the graduation traditions at Mount Holyoke. Either way, these classic sour drinks are easy to remember, easy to order, and easy to swallow.

WHISKEY SOUR (SMITH)

> 2 OZ. WHISKEY
> 1 TBSP. LEMON JUICE
> 1 TSP. SUGAR

Shake with ice and strain into Collins glass. Garnish with lemon slice and maraschino cherry.

AMARETTO SOUR
(MOUNT HOLYOKE)

2 OZ. AMARETTO

³/₄ OZ. LEMON JUICE

Shake well with ice and strain into Collins glass. Garnish with orange slice.

NOTE: If you're late for your date, sour mix is acceptable.

DANCE: **Foxtrot.**

Don't forget your stole and gloves.

MASSACHUSETTS MYSTERY MACHINE?

A popular urban legend has it that the members of the Five-College Consortium in Massachusetts's Pioneer Valley served as the inspiration for the five characters in the popular *Scooby-Doo* cartoon. Square-jawed Fred represents Amherst College; ditzy Daphne is Mount Holyoke; brainy Velma, Smith; reputed stoner Shaggy just dropped out of Hampshire; and the show's canine hero stands for UMass. Scrappy? Amherst Regional High School, of course.

Continuing in the grand tradition of Betty vs. Veronica and Ginger vs. Mary Ann, the Velma and Daphne designations vary depending on whom you talk to. (Go Velma!)

TaB: The Pink Lady

What deb can resist that pink can? The puffy typeface? The lowercase *a*? The lack of calories? In the '80s, few women could, especially those who needed to fit into white formal dresses.

The Coca-Cola Company introduced TaB, the first major diet cola, back in the 1960s, when Americans had begun to keep "tabs" on their weight. Contrary to an urban myth, TaB does not stand for "totally artificial beverage," though its use of the once-suspected-carcinogen saccharine did lessen its sweetness in the eyes of some. At the height of its popularity, TaB was available in every vending machine on the Wellesley campus. Students found that it came in handy for those all-night study sessions at the end of their first college semesters, when the pressure was on to race through final exams and catch the train in time for the big debut. Like Michael Jackson's original face, TaB's hard to find now, but still has a fiercely loyal following.

DANCE: Twist.

That's what hips are for.

The Wall of Shame
THE FUZZY NAVEL: OBVIOUSLY NAMED BY A MAN

Orange juice and peach schnapps—oh my! The syrupy-sweet super drink of the mid-'80s, the fuzzy navel, made the De Kuypers company a Croesus's fortune: their Peachtree schnapps was the first liqueur to sell more than one million cases in its first year of production. The fuzzy navel's success led to a Barry White greatest hits collection of other dubious peachy treats: the Slippery Nipple, the Woo Woo, and the Silk Panties. In short, the Tom Cruise *Cocktail* Drink Pantheon!

Slummin':
Misadventures on the
Preppy Periphery

"Rich people will travel far distances to look at poor people."
—DAVID BYRNE, LINER NOTES TO *STOP MAKING SENSE*
(1984)

To draw a line, some have observed, is already in some sense to surpass it. And with preppy drinking, the truth of this maxim is quite clear. The code of St. Grotlesex—the patron saint of preppydom—is all about decorum and doing the appropriate thing in the appropriate circumstances. But how is one to know the appropriate unless one first knows the verboten? The pressure-cooker demands of the private school as a "total institution"—the rigorous schedules, the stringent dress codes, the sermons about leadership—can petrify even the sturdiest and most vivacious into the dullest of bores. "Without some vulgarity," Raymond Chandler (Dulwich College, 1905) once wrote, "there is no complete man." And what are prep schools and liberal arts colleges if not places where men and women can become their complete selves? By its own topsy-turvy logic, then, preppiness requires one occasionally to experience life on the other side of the country club walls. And thus, the ineluctable appeal of that peculiar preppy pastime, slummin'.

Norman Mailer summed up the motivation to experience life off the Upper East Side grid best in his infamous 1957 essay, "The White Negro": in an age confronting nuclear peril, "the only life-giving answer is to accept the terms of death, to live with death as immediate danger, to divorce oneself from society, to exist without roots, to set out on that uncharted journey with the rebellious imperatives of

the self." In short, Mailer insists, one must adopt the code of
the hipster, which calls on one "to explore that domain of
experience where security is boredom and therefore sick-
ness." While '80s preppies lived with their own Cold War
nuclear face-off, they couldn't completely exist without
roots or society. Who wanted to risk getting cut off? Therefore, the '80s produced no one at the level of Slummin' Hall
of Famers Jack Kerouac (Horace Mann, '40) and William
Seward Burroughs II (Taylor School, '31). Still, the well-
heeled path along the wrong side of the tracks would prove
influential.

Slummin' drinks are only acceptable for the prep when
he or she is slummin'. As with all prep life, time and place
is everything. And when it comes time for slummin', who
knows where you'll end up? Alphabet City? Atlantic City?

A dive bar with no bathroom door? Will you come home with a Mohawk? A tattoo? A non-prep? *Will* you come home? Put on your ripped jeans—it's time to find out.

Boarding School Years

THE FORTY: THE EARLY YEARS OF
L. L. BEAN J.

"So one night I got really high on this cheap malt liquor and I pledged my love to her and the next day she ran off with a bass player named Ringo."

—SLUMMIN' ANDREW MCCARTHY TO ALLY SHEEDY ON JUST WHY LOVE SUCKS IN *ST. ELMO'S FIRE* (1985)

Malt liquor sipped through a straw hit big among early '90s preppies with a penchant for N.W.A. and Public Enemy. While the genealogy of the Scarsdale homie is a fascinating case of Norman Mailer's unexpected influence during the Bush 41 and Clinton eras, it remains outside of this book's purview. Nevertheless, malt liquor—American pilsner's obstreperous brother-in-law—has been circulating in prep circles from the beginning. Even before St. Ann's and Friends Seminary grads The Beastie Boys first fought for their right to party, one might imagine some Darien garden soirée during the hot summer of 1981. It's a weekend, the folks are in Maine, but you begged off going because you'd "already volunteered to help Bess entertain a group of visiting Soviet exchange students." A preppy soul band with white musicians wearing tuxedo-jacket-printed T-shirts is keeping it real. Some random people from the city show up who claim to know the drummer. They bring forties. It's all downhill from there.

The forty's popularity among preps is easy to explain: it's cheap, it's easily concealed (more so than a sixer), and it packs a heavy wallop. Perfect for hanging out in Central Park after school. The main brands are King Cobra, Olde English (O.E.), St. Ides, and Colt 45. The latter three are produced by Pabst owner G. Heileman; indeed, they taste a lot like Pabst, only with a heaviness and a bite that warms the back of the throat. Unlike regular 3 percent alcohol beer, however, these suckers contain up to 8 percent alcohol. So go easy, big fella, or else mo' money, mo' problems will be mo' like it.

WINE COOLERS: LIP SMACKERS

With their fruity flavors and bright colors, it makes sense that many girls' first alcohol experience came courtesy of two fuzzy old guys named Bartles and Jaymes. The competing brand, Seagram's, featured Mr. Moonlighting himself— Bruce Willis. Although preps usually resist the lures of advertising, '80s girls' schools were vulnerable to the homespun charm of Gallo's pitchmen from the plains. (As for Seagram's, well, Willis fans listened to *The Return of Bruno* only once.) Basically wine spritzers dressed in Esprit, the bubbly coolers were packed with sugar, which calmed preexam nerves even as it risked inducing a stomachache. Especially after you danced around your room to "Oh, What a Feeling."

THUNDERBIRD: "WHY, I HAVEN'T FELT THIS WOOZY SINCE THE LARCHMONT REGATTA"

As onetime prep-pop chanteuse Harriet Wheeler may have put it, here is where the story ends. Thunderbird, "the American Classic," is the skid row elixir par excellence, the booze of broken dreams. Like its distaff cousins Night Train and Boone's Wine, Thunderbird actually comes from Modesto's favorite sons, Ernest and Julio Gallo, who introduced the wine immediately following the repeal of Prohibition; these days, in the quest for middle-class respectability, they try to downplay this on the label.

With a sinister red-and-gold eagle seal that looks like the insignia for some fascist army, Thunderbird makes clear that it intends not to screw around: in this sense, consider it the G. Gordon Liddy of American wines. With your first sip of T-Bird—"citrus wine with natural flavors and caramel color"—the flavor socks you off your feet: imagine flat Bartles & Jaymes with a generous spiking of pure grain alcohol. In fact, there's *so much* alcohol (17.5 percent) that it almost floats above the citrus wine. T-Bird should come in bottles marked with skulls-and-crossbones. You uncap the metal lid and recall that time you got lost in Boston's Combat Zone and almost didn't make it out alive. You lift it toward your mouth and think of your mad aunt Kathryn, who spends her dotage commuting between Shaker Heights and Provincetown, and who's rumored to top off her glasses of wine with a little "something extra." You take your first sips and feel like Ray Milland in *Lost Weekend*; only cleaning fluid can be next on the menu. As the buzz kicks in, you're seized with morbid thoughts about people going blind from bad moonshine. In a mild panic, you squint to make sure you can see, but it's getting darker and darker . . .

Like revenge, Thunderbird is best served cold.

MD 20/20: MORE COLOR THAN A LILLY PULITZER CATALOG

Good ol' Mad Dog. If Larry Flynt were a vintner, he'd be crushing the grapes for this one. This fluorescent concoction, created by the "20/20 Wine Company" of Westfield, New York, looks just like Kool-Aid—the Jim Jones kind. Imagine melting Popsicles and mixing in a little Triaminic and white zinfandel, and you'll get a sense of the flavor. Described as "grape wine with citrus spirits," its flavor palate appears to have been adopted from a line-up of novelty sex lubricants: Mad Dog comes in Mango Lime, Orange Jubilee, Pacific Peach, Strawberry Rose, Key Lime Pie, Kiwi Lemon, and most intriguingly, Tangerine Dream. Like the music of the German prog-rock band that composed the sound track to *Risky Business*, this will put you into a heavy trance; after a few swigs, you'll feel as dreamy and pastel as Tom Cruise and Rebecca DeMornay on the Chicago El. Indeed, this is perhaps the only wine whose mouth feel can be described as "velour." Preps first drink this stuff when they're at boarding school: the cheap price (currently $2.00) and high alcohol content (13.5 percent) make it just the sort of thing to keep hidden when it comes time for the dreaded Thursday-morning room inspection. During your first semester of college, the rugby players who did post-grad years at boarding schools buy this stuff by the Jeepload. You were bound to join them on at least one occasion. This has no vintage; but, then again, what were you expecting?

PREP SCHOOL PROHIBITION

"All I ever did was to sell beer and whiskey to our best people."—AL CAPONE

Necessity, as they say, is the mother of invention, and nowhere was this truer than America under Prohibition. From 1919 to 1933, bathtub gin, wood alcohol highballs, and sundry other horrors were served up at speakeasies all across the land. Preps, of course, have always been receptive to the bootlegger: how else to explain the perennial assignment of *The Great Gatsby* in fourth-form English classes? During the 1980s, young preppy scofflaws carried on Jay's disreputable tradition, discovering illicit uses for the dorm soda vending machines.

Mountain Cactus

Pour one shot tequila into can of Mountain Dew. Swirl can.

College Years

BOONE'S FARM: THE COUNTRY HOUSE OF NO RETURN

On the campus of every preppy liberal arts college in New England, some mysterious gravitational pull tied them to-

Fahrenheit 151

Cuba Libre Libre

gether, usually during Orientation Week. Perhaps it was because one smoked, and the other two were looking to bum cigarettes. Either way, one of them hailed from Riverdale, one came from either Choate or Exeter, and the third was from some obscure California girl's school where coke-addled Paramount execs shipped their daughters. One had a Mercedes, another a Volkswagen, and at some point during college, one would get busted for possessing a fake ID. They were polished, they spoke good French, and they were loaded—on Boone's Farm Wine, of all things. No one quite understood why: They could drink anything they wanted, and the older Chi Psi gentlemen were always ready to run errands. But they ignored any suggestion that their taste was unseemly. Saturday nights, after the a cappella shows ended and before the big parties began, they sat in the dorm, listened to Huey Lewis (a.k.a. Hugh Anthony Clegg III, Lawrenceville '68), and enjoyed their Boone's in all its candy-flavored allure.

Using apple wine as a base, Boone's didn't aspire for the freakish extremes of such other nominal wines as MD 20/20 and Thunderbird. The bottles looked like regular old wine bottles, their labels featuring a rustic illustration of some sunny California apple orchard. Even the names tried to maintain some link, however tenuous, to nature: Snow Creek Berry, Wild Island, Blackberry Ridge—the whole package evinced a certain Joni Mitchell vibe. Mildly carbonated, extremely sweet (with a whopping twenty-four grams of sugar per glass), only mildly alcoholic (5 percent), this proto-Bartles & Jaymes was perhaps the only wine ever to contain partially hydrogenated soybean oil. The overall effect was like listening to the Go-Gos or putting on some Day-Glo bangle bracelets with your navy blue prep school uniform—and perhaps that explained Boone's appeal. The Boone's girls just wanted to have fun.

Jell-O is *not* preppy. It's horrifying. As a dessert, it embodies all the features of the better-living-in-Levittown aesthetic; unlike certain kinds of chocolate, it's bludgeoningly sweet; non-preps love to put unidentifiable floating objects in theirs; and most (or least) of all, it wiggles. Yet it does have one decisive virtue: properly prepared, it enables even the most bookish preps to imagine that they too go to rah-rah Big Ten schools, not the obscure Division III colleges that many happen to attend.

The key is the Jell-O shot, a dangerous alcoholic delicacy that by its very nature can be consumed only from a metal horse-imprint wastepaper basket in a loud room reeking of body odor and carnal desperation. The recipe itself is a model of simplicity:

> **JELL-O (COLOR-COORDINATE!)**
> **VODKA (CHEAP)**
> **BOILING WATER**

In a large metal pot, add 1 cup boiling water and 1 cup vodka to 1 packet of Jell-O. For every packet of Jell-O you use, add the equal proportions of water and vodka; for a decent party, you'll need about 10 boxes. Refrigerate overnight. (This is important. If you don't have overnight, you can put the mixture in the freezer, but you do have to give the mixture enough time to gel.) Once the Jell-O mixture has congealed, find a trusty wastepaper basket and line it with a garbage bag. Dump the Jell-O mixture into the lined basket

and hand out Dixie cups to all assembled. Sway to the music.

Since the Jell-O takes a while to digest, your bloodstream doesn't immediately absorb the alcohol; thus, if you indulge too quickly, a nasty surprise awaits. Know your limits. As your cheeks flush and you begin to stagger, grab yourself a chair and chat someone up about the Rose Bowl.

N . B . : Some people like to substitute Everclear 190 proof neutral grain spirits for vodka in their Jell-O shots. Since they have an unfortunate habit of dying as a result, we recommend against the practice.

The First Job

JÄGERMEISTER: SLOSHED BEHIND THE SHIELD OF ST. HUBERT

"This is the hunter's honor shield / So that he protects and preserves his game / He hunts like a sportsman, as is proper / The Creator in the creature he honors."

—THE JÄGERMEISTER LOGO, TRANSLATED FROM GERMAN

It happens all the time. Ever since your boarding school pal Elizabeth graduated from Amherst as an economics major, she's been spending seemingly endless nights toiling as an investment analyst at Drexel Burnham Lambert. Of course, it's still a few years before the big insider trading scandals close Drexel and free Elizabeth for good, but the mid-1980s economic rebound has not been good for Elizabeth's social life. It's her birthday. She's only turning twenty-five, but she's looking thirty. You and your friends kid her about the good old days but Elizabeth's not amused. She's planning on going back to the office. Maybe the economic malaise of your late–Carter era prep school days wasn't so bad after all.

Trip won the fifth-form oratory medal in '78. You let him coax Elizabeth out to Swell's on York Avenue. You start swiggin' the G&Ts, one after another, until the night's a blur. But Elizabeth's threatening to leave! On her birthday! It's time to bring out the heavy artillery. You order Jäger shots for all assembled, and preparing for the worst, you slug 'em down in one gulp. Nevertheless, you don't really feel that much drunker. You go back to G&Ts. Elizabeth goes back to work.

Face it: With an alcohol content of *only* 35 percent, Jägermeister has a much worse bark than bite. With its Gothic lettering and heavy metal persona, Jäger seems like the sort of drink to which Lemmy from Motorhead would wake, but it's not really so far removed from Pernod, the preppy equivalent of ouzo. Although more than a few preppy wits have spread the false rumor that this contains opium—no doubt owing to the beverage's dark brown color and reputation—Jäger is distinguished mostly by its strong note of anise, along with bitter overtones reminiscent of Campari. The bottle insignia is peculiar: The image looks like a reindeer thinking of a cross. Perhaps Rudolph dismayed with the commercialization of Christmas? Or perhaps something more archaic, a paean to that sporting ethos that reveals itself in duck motifs and good care of the family Labrador? Before we pull out our Elmer Fudd hats, however, let us not speculate too much further. While a fine shot for birthdays, bachelor parties, promotions, and layoffs, Jägermeister's somewhat overrated as the toughest drink you'll *ever* confront.

TEQUILA: THE HEADACHE THAT BUILDS CHARACTER

The national booze of Mexico, tequila is made from fermenting the sap found in the heart of the agave plant, which, contrary to a certain misconception, is not a cactus. Taste notwithstanding, tequila's not some cheap swill: Agaves take anywhere from seven to twelve years to grow to maturity, a sizable investment of time and resource. Sober preps typically keep away from tequila: The Tijuana ambience that surrounds the drink is scary enough, but it's the war stories about hellish hangovers that evoke a decisive Heisman response. Get any preppy drunk enough, however, and vestiges of masochism passed down through the boarding school collective unconscious come to light. Repressed memories of prep school life—cold showers at dawn, brutal lacrosse practices, orientation "trust-building" exercises—emerge from some dingy cigar box in the dark recesses of the reptilian brain. It's time for tequila shots.

A (sub)urban legend holds that tequila contains mescaline: after all, the spirit is related to another Mexican liquor called mescal. While there is nothing to that rumor—indeed, neither tequila nor mescal contain any illicit alkaloids—tequila shots are guaranteed to expand your mind, or at least pickle it. And your stomach, too—if you eat "the worm."

Certain ne'er-do-well boarding school chemists have been known through the decades to light smoke bombs outside the headmaster's residence. The formula is basic:

potassium nitrate and sugar in equal proportions. (There's a
reason why so many preps have worked for The Agency.)
Similarly, the formula for tequila shots is simple:

Pour a dash of salt on your hand.

Fill up a shot glass with tequila.

Lick your hand.

Down the tequila.

Bite down on a lime wedge.

Get a hangover.

Entrenched Adulthood

COLD TEA: NOT THE KIND THEY HAVE AT SMITH

It's 12:30 A.M. on Saturday night. You've been out carousing
with some old chums in Cambridge, Massachusetts. You've
hit Club Casablanca and the Oxford Ale House and you're
pretty happy. You're in the midst of recalling that one crazy
summer when one of your friends, then a senior at a Friends
school outside Philadelphia, was dating a junior (!) at Brown,

when—blam!—it's last call. You sigh. You live in New York City, where last call is just a rumor. But this is Massachusetts, a commonwealth with a long history of Puritan blue laws. Pilgrims be damned, you and your friends don't get to see each other that often. Not ready to call it a night, you ask if there are any after-hours clubs. Not like you've ever *been* to an after-hours club; you hear they exist from your New York friends daring enough to go to some no-man's-land called Alphabet City. But you have your tough New York image to uphold, even if you are just an editorial assistant at Dodd, Mead. "After hours?" Chip squints in confusion. Kip smiles. "How about Chinese food?"

Skip the Cantabridigian hails a taxi. That Cambridge has taxis is amusing to you, almost as amusing as the fact that New Haven has taxis. Of course, you're from Greenwich, Connecticut, where you have to make a phone call to get a cab. Kip directs the taxi to Chinatown, to a certain restaurant that shall go nameless because we don't want to deprive future drinkers from the pleasures to be found there. It's raining. The taxi lets you out in the storm. You love your life.

The restaurant has a faded pink and green décor. Your feet are wet through your Docksiders. The other people in the restaurant all appear to be Chinese, but you don't really think about this. You were talking about? Oh yes, that Brown junior. Providence is such an ironic name for that Rhode Island city. The waiter interrupts to get your order. Kip jumps in:

"Cold tea and a plate of ribs."

What's cold tea?

"You'll see." He winks.

The ribs arrive. And then the cold tea.

It comes in a generic Chinese restaurant teapot but when you touch it, it is indeed cold. One of your friends takes your porcelain teacup and fills it.

You sip. It's watered-down Busch.

It's not long before Kip is ordering another pot.

You sip some more.

An hour later, you and your friends are really hammered. Skip starts hitting Chip's upper arm. "Are you tough?" he demands. Chip just ignores him, but Skip continues punching. The waiter looks impatient. He doesn't want any trouble. Not when cold tea is being served. He brings the check.

Skip gets up to head to the bathroom but instead walks into a giant plant and knocks it over. The waiter announces that the restaurant is closed and follows you to the door. There will be no more cold tea tonight.

CHINESE RESTAURANT FREE HOUSE WINE: SOME DUMPLINGS WITH YOUR CHABLIS?

If watered-down beer wasn't your thing, there were other, legal alternatives. When Thai food became popular among preps in the 1980s, some Chinese restaurants tried to remain current by adding spicy Szechuan cuisine to their menus. Others, with a better sense of their patrons, took a more direct route: free wine with your entree. Hence, the garish old-style establishments—the kind where Chuck Norris pummeled the crap out of drug dealers in flicks like

An Eye for An Eye (1981)—found themselves teeming on Friday nights with young preppies looking to get loaded on the cheap. While the greasy food itself naturally limited how often even the most iron-stomached could indulge, the MSG at least brought out some nuances in the Chardonnay.

POLYNESIAN: DRINKS TO MAKE YOU UKE

Indeed, when it comes to Chinese restaurants, why bother to eat at all? At their best, Chinese restaurant bars are stages for over-the-top performances apt to make Jack Palance's look like masterpieces of understatement. Although the tweedier preps grimace, others partake in this 1950s institution without shame. Victor "Trader Vic" Bergeron invented the Mai Tai in 1944 and opened his first restaurant in Seattle in 1949. Eventually even The Plaza Hotel in Manhattan had a Trader Vic's. (It was a popular date spot with the Princeton Country Day School set.) Even if a little on the sweet side, a well-prepared Polynesian drink appeals to the enduring prep affinity for bright colors and sky-high alcohol content. Not to mention Don Ho.

BLUE HAWAIIAN

Greg Brady meets Elvis!

1 OZ. LIGHT RUM

1 OZ. BLUE CURACAO

1 OZ. PINEAPPLE JUICE

1 TBSP. CREME OF COCONUT

Shake ingredients with ice and strain into a chilled cocktail glass. Garnish with pineapple slice and a cherry. Umbrella optional.

MAI TAI

Loosen *your* tie.

1 OZ. DARK RUM

¼ OZ. CURACAO

1 TBSP. LIME JUICE

1 TSP. GRENADINE

1 TSP. SUGAR

Shake with ice. Strain over ice into an old-fashioned glass. Garnish with a pineapple and cherry.

SCORPION BOWL

It stings.

2 OZ. VODKA

2 OZ. GIN

3 OZ. RUM

3 OZ. GRENADINE

3 OZ. PINEAPPLE JUICE

3 OZ. ORANGE JUICE

If you're ordering it in a Chinese restaurant (recommended), you'll get it in the namesake "scorpion bowl." Since no prep owns one of these, substitute the biggest damn goblet in your china cabinet. Fill your receptacle of choice half full of ice. Stir in the alcohol and juice. Garnish with all the citrus in your fruit bowl.

SINGAPORE SLING

The zing will make you sing and feel like a king but check for a ring if you want a fling.

2 OZ. GIN

1/2 OZ. WILD CHERRY BRANDY

1 TBSP. LEMON JUICE

1 TSP. SUGAR

Shake well with ice and strain into Collins glass. Add ice and soda water to fill. Stir and serve with colored straws.

ZOMBIE

They're not kidding. Be sure you have cab fare home.

1 OZ. LIGHT RUM

1 OZ. DARK RUM

1 OZ. JAMAICAN RUM

1/2 OZ. 151-PROOF RUM

2 OZ. PINEAPPLE JUICE

1 OZ. LIME JUICE

1 OZ. ORANGE JUICE

DASH OF GRENADINE

Shake ingredients with ice. Serve in Collins glass with straw and garnish with pineapple and orange slices and a cherry.

NEW YORK CITY TAP WATER

It's what you drink when you stumble home at five in the morning. Fill your glass; drop the needle on *Some Girls* by The Rolling Stones. Pop an aspirin and curl up on the couch as the new dawn fades. Mick sings of sex and lies and dirty dreams, but they seem somehow always to elude you. As you drift into slumber, you realize that the alumni phone-a-thon is tomorrow. . . .

The Wall of Shame

All of the above.

The Sun's
Past Half-Mast:
Brunchtime Buoys

*"Who wants to suck down a few Bloody Marys at St.
Elmo's on me?"*

—JULES (DEMI MOORE) TO GROUP, *ST. ELMO'S FIRE* (1985)

For the 1980s prep the week ends—and begins—with drinking. Despite their card-carrying Episcopalian tendencies, preps on Sunday are not sipping the wine at church, they're downing Bloody Marys at brunch. A must on the social schedule, brunch—a.k.a. socially sanctioned daytime drinking—has replaced the Sunday family dinner as a leisurely time to rehash the events the night before, see old boarding school chums, and partake of the hair of the dog. (Usually a golden retriever.) It's a fine way to skirt outdated blue laws.

Although some roll their eyes at brunch as a newfangled pastime of the trendy '80s, it's been around for a long time. The August 1, 1896, issue of the aptly named *Punch* magazine instructs, "To be fashionable nowadays we must 'brunch.'" As with almost everything prep, Sunday brunch is most popular on the coasts—preferably the North Atlantic. Although brunch was apparently served as early as 1933 at Chicago's Ambassador Hotel to bi-coasters making overnight stops in the Windy City during train trips, brunch did not gain a real foothold in the general culture until after World War II.

Nowadays, of course, no self-respecting prep gets up early on Sunday. And very few self-respecting preps actually cook. But even preppies have to eat sometime. After a half-assed attempt at the crossword, it's time to meet the gang. Brunch is an afternoon affair held at a SoHo restau-

THE TAILGATE

"We want to follow the pattern set for us. We go to an Ivy League college. . . . Then we go back and have tailgate parties and drink Bloody Marys."
—A GROTON SENIOR QUOTED BY *THE NEW YORK TIMES*
  (MAY 27, 1984)

It's a quaint misnomer: how can it be "*the* game" when the Ivy League doesn't even rate for today's college football fans? But some say the annual Harvard-Yale game—which celebrated its one hundredth anniversary on November 19, 1984—was the birthplace of that modern football fixture, the tailgate party. Indeed, the spectators attend this self-important contest as much (if not more) for the pre-game as for the game itself. And no tailgate party is complete without alcohol. Any of our brunch choices are acceptable. But this is not your run-of-the-NFL Foxboro Stadium tailgate party! At the Yale Bowl, it's about linen, china, and crystal—raccoon coats optional. Pack accordingly.

rant (for city preps) or at the club (for city preps and country preps alike); an appropriately kitschy diner is acceptable for those still slumming from the night before. If you must attend a brunch at someone's home or—heaven help you—host one yourself, don't expect to eat—or serve—much. If you're lucky, everyone will still be recovering from the night before and will want to keep it light. Accordingly, some hosts (and guests) will consider a Bloody Mary their main entrée. If you must provide more, go French. Spread your Hudson's Bay Point Blanket out on Grandmother's old Oriental and pass the baguettes, croissants, and brie. *Voila!* It's the Boston Riviera. If you're serving mimosas, screwdrivers, or salty dogs, the fruit juices should be enough. And with the Bloody Mary, there's always the celery stick.

Yes, the preppiest cocktail of them all actually has some nutritional value, not to mention a nickname. (Preppies love nicknames.) Though we have seen the Bloody make appearances at places other than Sunday brunch, few self-respecting preppies can face the rest of the week without one. So hold your nose, chums, and learn to love it.

BLOODY MARY

The preppiest of all drinks, and that's saying something. As with most lore about the origins of cocktails, the stories conflict about who invented the Bloody Mary and how it got its name. Most agree that this American classic was invented in the 1920s by Fernand Petiot, a bartender at Harry's New York Bar in Paris. The initial version of the drink contained just the essentials—vodka and tomato juice. Did a guy in the bar suggest the drink be called "Bloody Mary" because it reminded him of the Bucket of Blood Club in Chicago and a girl he knew there named Mary? Seems unlikely to us. The more likely namesake is Mary I of England, daughter of Henry VIII, known as "Bloody Mary" because she killed a lot of Protestants. No wonder this is the preppy drink: Mary was a legacy, after all, and by naming their favorite drink after her, the Protestant prep majority got to indulge their penchant for irony.

As an indication of his high status in the prep pantheon, we've seen the mixologist Petiot referred to by not one but *two* nicknames: Pete and Fred. When he moved to New York in 1934 he brought the drink to the King Cole Bar at the St. Regis Hotel in Manhattan. The hotel, being the St. Regis, didn't see the irony and wanted to change the name to "Red Snapper." Thank God it didn't stick. Supposedly, New Yorkers found Petiot's stripped-down vodka-and-tomato-juice drink too bland, so our bartender added salt, black pepper, cayenne pepper, Worcestershire sauce, and lemon juice. Pete/Fred preferred Manhattans.

By the way, the Bloody Mary is the only acceptable drink to make in large quantity. In that case, you would refer to it as "a batch of Bloodies." Punches are for children's birthday parties, not preppies. You will see many variations of the Bloody Mary but for the true prep there is only one original.

1½ OZ. VODKA

2 OZ. TOMATO JUICE

THREE DROPS TABASCO SAUCE

FOUR DASHES WORCESTERSHIRE SAUCE

ONE SPLASH LEMON JUICE

SALT AND BLACK PEPPER, TO TASTE

Shake with ice, then strain into old-fashioned glass. Garnish with celery stick and lemon slice.

ACCESSORY: *A hangover*
ACTIVITY: *None*
DON'T: *Drink after 3:00 P.M.!*

NOTE: **Beware the oversized Bloody!**

TO MIX OR NOT TO MIX?

Along with the Sour Sisters (see Chapter 4, "Come Out Swinging"), the Bloody Mary is the only drink for which it is acceptable to use a mix. The preppy choice? Mr. and Mrs. T (no relation to the other Mr. T., of course). According to the company history, Herb and June Taylor "suffered through many bland Bloody Marys at local restaurants until they resolved to do something about it!" Their Bloody mix debuted in Los Angeles in 1960, where a vice president of American Airlines tasted one. Herb and June's concoction was soon flying the friendly skies. The rest is history. The couple retired very rich; preppies continued drinking. Everybody is happy.

BLOODY DRINKING IS NOT DEMOCRATIC

These days, it's become fashionable for restaurants serving brunch to feature "Bloody Mary Bars" where patrons can "customize" their drinks. Drinkers are adding everything from black- or green-stuffed olives, onions, dill pickle spears, peppers, baby corn, artichoke hearts, hearts of palm, cold boiled shrimp, carrot sticks, cherry tomatoes, cucumber slices, mushroom buttons, and water chestnuts to their Bloodies. While some tailoring is necessary for a new suit, your cocktail is *not* a salad.

BLAME CANADA

The Bloody Caesar was invented in Canada in 1969; since then, it has become a Canadian tradition up there with Dudley Do-Right and rolling oneself over Niagara Falls in a wooden barrel. The key ingredient in the Bloody Caesar is clam juice or Clamato, a tomato clam cocktail seasoned with "secret" spices. Although the Bloody Caesar's Canadian popularity isn't matched in the States, it seems that Clamato, available only in the United States, Canada, Mexico, and the Caribbean, is the drink that brings the continent together.

We include the following variations of the Bloody Mary for informational purposes only. We in no way condone them. In addition, some Bloody Mary recipes call for Absolut Peppar, a flavored vodka introduced in the United States in 1986. To that we say, absolute-ly not!

Bloody Maria: Substitute tequila for vodka
Red Snapper: Substitute gin for vodka
Bloody Bull: Add beef bouillon
Bloody Caesar: Add clam juice

N O T E : **Preps** *never* **drink Virgin Marys.**

While there is really only one preppy brunch drink, the Bloody Mary, we realize that there are times when a bloody is just too, well, bloody. Therefore we have also included a champagne drink (the mimosa), a prime pick of preppy hardware (the screwdriver), and a classic hangover helper (the salty dog).

MIMOSA

"Champagne and orange juice is a great drink. The orange improves the champagne. The champagne definitely improves the orange."

—H.R.H. PRINCE PHILIP, DUKE OF EDINBURGH

Champagne, while upper class, is not itself a preppy drink. (See Chapter 8, "The Wrath of Grapes.") Orange juice, while healthy, is also not a preppy drink. But together, think Orangina with a kick! And it's so much easier to prepare than a Bloody Mary—perfect for tailgating at Myopia Hunt Club. The champagne should be dry; the O.J. should be chilled; the croquet wickets should be in place.

CHAMPAGNE

ORANGE JUICE

Pour equal parts chilled champagne and orange juice into white-wine glass; stir.

ACCESSORY: *Cole Porter tunes*
ACTIVITY: *Tailgate picnic*
DON'T: *Drink if there are Bloodies on hand*

SCREWDRIVER

Take the vodka from a Bloody Mary and the orange juice from a mimosa, and the result is hardware fit to ensure your weekend restoration. A man in Iran had a plan when a swizzle stick was hard to come by on the oil rig where he was working. He used his trusty screwdriver to stir his drink. That's what we like to call Yankee ingenuity.

2 OZ. VODKA

ORANGE JUICE

Pour vodka into Collins glass over ice. Orange juice to fill and stir.

ACCESSORY: *Stirrer*
ACTIVITY: *Sneering at the Mergers and Acquisitions page in the* Times
DON'T: *Get hammered*

SALTY DOG

Brunch is all about the hair of the dog so it makes sense to order a drink named after one. This drink combines two preppy motifs: animals and the sea. Preps love their animals, particularly horses and ducks but dogs are OK, too. Preps also love anything related to the salty sea. And they like to frequent bars in sailing towns like Marblehead, Manchester-by-the-Sea and Newport, with nautical names like The Blue Parrot. It makes them feel authentic, like Gloucester fishermen, even though their day on the boat was spent in leisure, not commerce. (Real fishermen always wear socks.)

If you're really hungover and you just can't stomach a Bloody anything, then the Salty Dog is for you.

> 2 OZ GIN
>
> ¼ TSP. SALT
>
> GRAPEFRUIT JUICE

Pour gin and salt into Collins glass over ice. Grapefruit juice to fill. Stir.

NOTE: **Vodka may be substituted for the gin.**

ACCESSORY: *Sunburnt, freckled nose*
ACTIVITY: *Yacht club hijinks*
DON'T: *Give any to the family Lab*

DOG DAYS

Since 1979, The Black Dog Tavern in Vineyard Haven on Martha's Vineyard has been selling T-shirts with their black dog logo on the front and the year and restaurant name on the back. Although preps typically eschew "legible clothing" except for the odd monogram, the Dog is an exception—provided the date on yours is pre-Clinton; otherwise, don't even bother wearing it.

The Wall of Shame
WITH CHEESE?: THE KIR ROYALE

Every brunch menu has it, but no preppy ever orders it. Named after Felix Kir, the mayor of Dijon, France. Hold it—and the mustard.

SEVEN

At the Club:
The Old Guard

*"Here we have no poor losers, bounders, mockers, or cads—
and if one should take a cocktail too many and speak with
loosened tongue, nobody outside is the wiser."*

—DIXON WECTER, *THE SAGA OF AMERICAN SOCIETY*

In his recent book *Bowling Alone*, Robert Putnam decried the decline of the voluntary association, but Putnam sure hasn't been hanging around preppies, one group for whom "voluntary association" has been a defining feature from the start. While preppies never bowl—unless to fulfill their sixth-form spring athletic requirements—they like to go clubbing. But not with the Peter Gatien bridge-and-tunnel set. Nope, preps join clubs to play golf and tennis, sail, meet business connections, engage in witty repartee, and drink. And not necessarily in that order.

It makes sense. Preps grow up at the club; they go to schools and camps that function like c"lubs. At preppy colleges, they join clubs themselves—whether they be select associations such as Harvard's Porcellian Club, eating clubs such as Princeton's Ivy Club, or secret societies such as Yale's **[NAME WITHHELD]**. And when it comes to athletics, they play club sports.

> *"Non-curricular opportunities include aviation ground school, choral groups, Outing Club, Photography Club, drama, water safety certification, drivers education, and the Society of Sceptics Club."*—BLAIR ACADEMY, BLAIRSTOWN, NEW JERSEY

After graduation, you might join the university club if you were a young prep from the American hinterlands seeking to make your name in Gotham. It wasn't always easy to get in, though: to join the Yale Club, for instance, a diploma with the *Lux et Veritas* wouldn't quite cut it. A member had to propose you for membership, another had to second you, and the membership committee had to give you the approval. You *definitely* needed a drink after that.

If you were a city prep who'd been in town for a few years, you might join a metropolitan club. The first in America was the Philadelphia Club, founded in 1830, and located since 1850 at the corner of 13th and Walnut Streets in the City of Brotherly Love. The Century Club in New York and the Somerset Club in Boston soon followed. Of course, drinking was a part of the city club scene from the first. The city clubs grew out of the seventeenth-century London coffeehouse scene. The St. James district, where the clubs flourished, was known simply as "clubland."

The first country club in America was the eponymous Country Club, established in 1882 at Brookline, Massachusetts, and still operating today. At a time when preps—or proto-preps—were city creatures, going to the club was like going to the country. The country club became a solid fixture of that first great age of preppydom, the 1920s. It's where the boater hat and flapper contingent played nine holes while their caddies nursed their winter dreams. In fact, in 1929, the number of country clubs in America hit an all-time peak of 4,500.

After World War II, as the trillium fields of suburbia became a stomping ground for a generation of new preps, the club scene became big once again. The mid-1950s marked an explosion in golf course construction. And where there was a golf course, there was an accompanying bar. Yet the gray-flannel glory days didn't last. By the end of the 1960s, the club scene was in crisis. Preps who would've joined clubs were scared away by the jacket-and-necktie ethos. As the recession of the early 1970s took hold, clubs started to close or move into cheaper headquarters.

But the 1980s brought a club renaissance. The Thursday night happy hours became hot once again; the foozball tables in the Grill Room got some new action. For preps confronted with the froo-froo intricacies of trendy '80s cocktails, the club was a comfortable bar away from home where the usual standards still applied, even as time went by.

Although preps diversify in their financial portfolios, they usually belong just to one club, maybe to two or three at most, but never to dozens. That's ostentation. Besides, if you belong only to one club, the bartender always knows your drink.

So whether you're a city prep or a country prep, here are recipes for the Brooks Brothers—classic, investment-grade drinks that build character.

Neatness Counts: Scotch and?

Let's cut to the chase. If you've reached the age where you're joining clubs, there's a good chance you want to keep things as simple—and potent—as possible. So you probably order your booze straight—or "neat," as they say. Your main pick is undoubtedly some form of whiskey, most likely scotch; sometimes bourbon or Canadian; hardly ever rye. You go for the single-malt scotches on occasion, but when you do, you keep to the Glenlivet. Those smoky Laphroaigs are a young man's game.

That's not to rule out variety, though. After all, whiskey comes from a Gaelic word meaning "water of life," and a little H_2O never hurt anything.

WHISKEY AND WATER

 Just a splash.

> 2 OZ. WHISKEY
> WATER

Add whiskey to old-fashioned glass and add water to fill. Garnish with a lemon twist.

WHISKEY ON THE ROCKS

 The ice soothes the whiskey burn; thus, less preppy than water.

> 2 OZ. WHISKEY

Add whiskey to old-fashioned glass and add ice cubes.

WHISKEY AND SODA

 Least preppy, but still preppy: the soda risks reducing the whiskey into a soft drink.

> 2 OZ. WHISKEY
> SODA WATER

Add whiskey to old-fashioned glass and add soda to fill. Garnish with a lemon twist.

MARTINI

Prep fathers tend to be men of few words. So, too, are we about the martini. Hasn't too much already been said?

1 ½ OZ. GIN
¾ OZ. DRY VERMOUTH

Pour gin into shaker over ice, then add vermouth. Stir vigorously until cold. Strain immediately into chilled cocktail glass. Serve with olive or lemon twist.

DRY MARTINI

1 ⅔ OZ. GIN
⅓ OZ. DRY VERMOUTH

See martini directions.

EXTRA-DRY MARTINI

1 ¾ OZ. GIN

¼ OZ. DRY VERMOUTH

See martini directions.

VODKA MARTINI

Less preppy, but still acceptable, especially in the summer.

1 ½ OZ. VODKA

¾ OZ. DRY VERMOUTH

See martini directions.

NOTE: **Preppies do not drink sweet martinis.**

GIBSON

"He ordered a Gibson and shouldered his way in between two other men at the bar, so that if she should be watching from the window she would lose sight of him."

—JOHN CHEEVER, "THE FIVE-FORTY-EIGHT"

Charles Dana Gibson, the artist known for the Gibson Girl, was also known as a potential originator of this drink. A member of The Players Club in Manhattan from 1891 to 1903, it is said to have originated there on a day when the bartender was out of olives.

1 2/3 OZ. GIN

1/3 OZ. DRY VERMOUTH

See martini directions; substitute cocktail onions for olives.

Clubhouse Row

"In the Yale Club they met a group of their former classmates who greeted the visiting Dean vociferously. Sitting in a semi-circle of lounges and great chairs, they had a highball all around."

—F. SCOTT FITZGERALD, "MAY DAY"

The section of land between Vanderbilt Avenue and Avenue of the Americas, from 45th Street to 39th Street, could possibly comprise the preppiest section of Manhattan Island, if not the United States. Not only can you find flagship stores for J. Press (7 East 44th Street), Brooks Brothers (346 Madison Avenue), Paul Stuart (356 Madison Avenue), and young upstart J. Crew (347 Madison Avenue), but classic prep hotels The Algonguin (59 West 44th Street) and The Royalton (44 West 44th Street) are waiting nearby with their bars well stocked. The old New Yorker offices are located at 123 West 43rd Street (right down the way from both the New York Yacht Club and the Century Club). And to top it off, the main alumni clubs in the preppy college world make their base there as well.

In the early 1980s, after years of decline following the 1960s, the university clubhouse scene perked up with a vengeance. At the Princeton Club, for example, nearly 20 percent of the class of 1981 joined upon graduation—the largest percentage ever. Graduation needn't spell the end of college social life; a club cocktail party happens every month. Although the N.Y.U. Club in the old *New Yorker* building closed its doors in 1989, Clubhouse Row was a fine place for the 1980s prep to jitterbug.

THE PRINCETON CLUB

15 West 43rd Street
www.princetonclub.com

AFFILIATE CLUBS: Columbia and Barnard. Until 1974, Columbia University Club of New York occupied a building across the street at 4 West 43rd Street, but sagging memberships led the club to sell the building to the Unification Church—a.k.a. "The Moonies." Today, that building is co-occupied by the Unification Church and the Church of Scientology.

CLUB BAR: The Tiger Grill and Bar.

COMMENTS: It's surprising that Princeton would go with the ugly modernist building (which gives off more of a Whitney Griswold–era Yale vibe), but the club compensates hard inside. According to the membership application, "Members and their guests are asked to respect the sensibilities of other members by striving to uphold standards of dignity and good taste in wardrobe selections." Expect to slug 'em down with Old Guard in bright orange sport coats with faux-tiger stripes.

30 West 44th Street
www.pennclub.org

AFFILIATE CLUBS: Vassar. Until the opening of the club in 1994, Penn was an affiliate of the Princeton Club. ("A century long dream . . . a vibrant reality," reads the club brochure.) The current site is the home of the pre-1915 Yale Club.

CLUB BAR: The Grill Room.

COMMENTS: Although Penn ties with Columbia as the least preppy of the Ivies, the authors had the good luck of visiting the club as a special alumni sign-up drive was in session. Our tour guide showed us the second-floor Presidents and Provosts Room—hope yet for the world's academic administrators, perhaps—and pointed out the window toward the Harvard Club across the street. "We like to think that we look down on the 'other' club," she joked. A little distracted, she then called our attention to the stained glass in the dining room where we were standing: "It's an exact replica of the stained glass that can be found in the library at *Penn State!*" A middle-aged fellow on our tour winced; he and his wife did not sign up afterwards.

24 East 39th Street
www.williamsclub.org

AFFILIATE CLUBS: Albany Law School; Amherst (admittedly, no *real* Jeff would join); Babson; Baruch; Bates; Bennington; Bentley; Bowdoin; Bucknell; Carleton; Case Western Reserve; Colby; Colgate; Connecticut College; Denison; Dickinson; Drexel; Georgetown; Goucher; Hamilton; Hobart and William Smith; INSEAD; Kenyon; Lawrence U.; Marymount; Massachusetts Institute of Technology; Middlebury; Mount Holyoke; New York Law School; Ohio State; Rensselaer Polytechnic Institute; Rutgers; Seton Hall; Sewanee; Sienna; Skidmore; Smith; St. John's University; St. Lawrence; SUNY Albany; Susquehanna U.; Trinity; Tufts; Union; University College London; University of Connecticut; University of North Carolina; University of Rochester; Wesleyan

CLUB BAR: Purple Cow Grill Room. Bartender Orlando Ventura's been there for years.

COMMENTS: The big-tent approach to affiliation reduces the Williams Club's preppy cred in quality just as it paradoxically increases it in quantity, yet the clubhouse has the charming run-down splendor of a London hotel. It would make a good set for a Stanley Kubrick movie. So would Williamstown, Massachusetts, come to think of it. (*The Shining?*)

THE HARVARD CLUB

27 West 44th Street
www.hcny.com

AFFILIATE CLUBS: Are you kidding?

CLUB BAR: The Grill Room.

COMMENTS: Lots of wood.

THE CORNELL CLUB

6 East 44th Street
www.cornellclubnyc.com

AFFILIATE CLUBS: Brown, Colgate, Duke, Georgetown, Stanford, Tulane

CLUB BAR: Big Red Tap & Grill

COMMENTS: With its aggie school and Cayuga Lake
hari-kiri rituals, Cornell is on the less preppy side of the
Ivy spectrum, but the university's ornate clubhouse
nicely ups its prep quotient.

THE YALE CLUB

50 Vanderbilt Avenue (at East 44th Street)
www.yaleclubnyc.org

AFFILIATE CLUBS: Dartmouth College and University
of Virginia. When the club adopted a casual Friday
dress code in the late '90s, old Eli stalwarts blamed the
bad influence of the thugs from Big Green.

CLUB BARS: Main Bar and The Grill Room. Yale Club Lager served on draught.

COMMENTS: The world's largest college clubhouse, and site of countless drinking scenes in Fitzgerald short stories. In the 1980s, the Yale Club was the third largest private club in the United States.

MANHATTAN

"Mr. Henlein took me to a place of refreshment twenty-five years ago, and I drank two Manhattan cocktails that made me so sick and dizzy that I've never liked the stuff since."

—JOHN CHEEVER, "THE SORROWS OF GIN"

BIG THREE COCKTAILS

Although the preppy authenticity of these drinks remains somewhat controversial, their vermouth speaks in their favor. Garnish all three with sprigs of ivy.

Harvard Cocktail

1 1/2 OZ. BRANDY

3/4 OZ. SWEET VERMOUTH

1 DASH BITTERS

2 TSP. LEMON JUICE

1 TSP. GRENADINE

Shake with ice and strain into cocktail glass.

Yale Cocktail

1 1/2 OZ. GIN

1/2 OZ. DRY VERMOUTH

1 DASH BITTERS

1 TSP. BLUE CURACAO

Stir with ice and strain into cocktail glass.

Princeton Cocktail

1 OZ. GIN

1 OZ. DRY VERMOUTH

1 TBSP. LIME JUICE

Stir with ice and strain into cocktail glass.

Invented at the Manhattan Club in New York City in 1874 when the future mother of Winston Churchill gave a party for the newly elected governor of New York.

> 1 1/2 OZ. WHISKEY
>
> 3/4 OZ. SWEET VERMOUTH
>
> 1 DASH BITTERS (OLD SCHOOL INGREDIENT)

Stir with ice and strain into cocktail glass. Serve with a cherry.

DRY MANHATTAN

A slightly preppier version of the above.

> 1 1/2 OZ. WHISKEY
>
> 3/4 OZ. DRY VERMOUTH
>
> 1 DASH BITTERS

Stir with ice and strain into cocktail glass. Serve with an olive.

NOTE: **Although Armani lounge lizard Richard Gere was partial to dry Manhattans in *American Gigolo* (1980), his preferences do not diminish the essential preppiness of the drink.**

ROB ROY

The Manhattan for those who insist on scotch.

1 ½ OZ. SCOTCH

¾ OZ. SWEET VERMOUTH

1 DASH ORANGE BITTERS

Stir with ice and strain into cocktail glass.

OLD-FASHIONED

"I remember: the club lounges before dinner dimly lighted and opulent like the church; the wool rugs absorbing footsteps; the lined damask curtains lapping thickly across tall, leaded-glass windows. The adults drank old-fashioneds. The fresh-haired children subsisted on bourbon-soaked maraschino cherries, orange slices, and ice cubes."

—ANNIE DILLARD, *AN AMERICAN CHILDHOOD*

To sip an old-fashioned is to imagine what it was like to drink at Pittsburgh's Duquesne Club during the last days of American steel. Outside, the Pirates were winning the World Series; the Steelers were victorious at the Super Bowl. Inside, the president of Gulf Oil would be standing on your left; Alcoa's CEO would be sitting on your right; and straight ahead, white-haired Jones and Laughlin executives would be making small talk about the Shady Side–Ellis mixer that their children would be attending that Friday. Bitters predominate; a hint of sweetness creeps through.

The old-fashioned was created at The Pendennis Club in Louisville, Kentucky.

1 CUBE SUGAR

2 DASHES BITTERS

1 TSP. WATER

2 OZ. WHISKEY

Add sugar cube, bitters, and water to old-fashioned glass and mash together with back of spoon. Add one ice cube, whiskey, and lemon twist. Stir. Garnish with slices of orange and lemon and a cherry. Serve with a swizzle stick.

"The Academy is 'old-fashioned' where it really counts: in the standards and examples it sets for students in the areas of personal conduct, integrity, diligence and appearance. It is, at the same time, 'modern' in such important aspects as curriculum, facilities, equipment, and adaptability."—ST. JOHNSBURY ACADEMY, ST. JOHNSBURY, VERMONT

WARD EIGHT

Invented at Boston's Locke-Ober Café in 1898. Some of the bartender's regular customers were members of the Hendrick's Club, the Democratic political organization of a candidate running to represent Ward Eight in the State House, so he created this drink for them the night before the election.

When in Boston, head up Route 1 to the Continental Restaurant in Saugus and ask for Jimmy, the ninety-two-year-old bartender. He'll set you up.

> 2 OZ. WHISKEY
>
> 1 TBSP. LEMON JUICE
>
> 1 TSP. SUGAR
>
> 1 TSP. GRENADINE

Shake with ice and strain into red-wine glass filled with cracked ice. Add slices of orange and lemon and a cherry. Serve with straws. Or not.

The Wall of Shame
SEVEN AND SEVEN = ZERO

Preppies drink Seagram's Seven Crown neat or with water, not with 7-Up.

EIGHT

The Wrath of Grapes:
In Vino Preppitas, or A Tale
of Two Cities

"I might drink a little wine or champagne socially, but never to the point of getting high."

—BROOKE SHIELDS, *ON YOUR OWN* (1985)

Throughout the years, a quarrel has been raging between two forces, which we shall call "Rome" and "Paris," a conflict that found preppies stuck in the middle as the 1980s began. Rome is about order punctuated by bacchanalia; preps in sixth-form Latin learn from Suetonius all about how the twelve Caesars loved their wine in moderate immoderation, even if they gasp at Caligula's torturous excesses. For the Roman, wine loosens inhibitions; it clears the vision and loves the world. Rome is the raucous spirit of Peter Ustinov bellowing into the crowd, "Drink, drink!" The symbol of Rome, therefore, is the jug wine—the big, unpretentious, non-vintage bottle of wine created from the juice of a slew of different grape varietals. In the United States, such wines had names like "Hearty Burgundy" and "Chablis of California." Although the wines had nothing in common with the European versions, American winemakers adopted European names because Europe's best wines historically had been associated with their locations of production.

Paris, by contrast, stands back, sniffs, and adjusts its beret. Paris is all about reserve, both in the emotional and upscale vintner's senses. Instead of dissolving social boundaries, the wine symbolized by Paris becomes a marker of distinction, of good manners and the refined palate. Paris casts a suspicious eye on bustling crowds and carnival excess. For Paris, wine stands in counterpoint to festivity; it is not the way to achieve it. It prefers the subtle pleasures of private life: the salon, the five-course dinner, the dry, sparkling champagne to match the dry, sparkling conversation. The jug wine draws a grimace: For Paris, the only wine worth its bottle is the vintage varietal, the wine identified by its grape and its year. The *vin du table* loses out to the *vin du marque*.

The battle is ancient, and probably irreconcilable. But the early 1980s marked the moment when Paris made decisive strides toward victory. True, Rome still had its influence: In fact, during the early '80s, jug wine sales reached a peak of 105 million cases a year. As the spirit of Paris increasingly set the tone over the next decade or so, however, those sales would drop off an astonishing 50 percent. Meanwhile, a flood of cheap and decent varietals from Australia, Argentina, Chile, and—eventually—South Africa deluged the U.S. market. Today, the classic jug wine, the spirit of Rome, holds on, but barely; the ruins of the imperium are a curiosity for tourists.

Of course, it would be foolish necessarily *to favor* the Roman style over the Parisian. For the 1980s prep, Rome and Paris are both essential influences that complement each other, even as they stand in tension. So how did the preppy manage to reconcile his or her competing allegiances? What was—and what is—preppy wine drinking?

Aldo Cella is dead; chill a Cella!

Starting out Right:
Appetizer Wines and Sherries

Although the distinctions among wines to enjoy before, during, and after dinner have broken down, preppies have typically enjoyed a glass of Lillet or sherry before meals. The former, a proprietary blend of wine, liquors, fruits, and herbs, was first created in France in 1886. At the height of the preppy era in 1981, nearly 80 percent of the Lillet produced was exported to the United States. And preppies were the market.

Sherries—which find their origin in Jerez de la Frontera in southwestern Spain—are wines infused with brandy to halt their fermentation; the resulting blends contain about 20 percent alcohol per volume. Their stateside popularity peaked circa 1972, yet an especially anglophilic subset of preps continues to keep them a viable drinking option. After all, sherry is more or less the official drink of eccentric old Oxbridge historians who own cats with names like Lord Haldane. As the wine-drinking world has climbed aboard the Merlot-nay bandwagon (see page 142), some wine spectators have come to consider fine sherry the best wine deal around: a top-drawer sherry sells these days for well under $20.

Among pre-dinner sherries, *finos* tend to be light and dry, *Manzanillas* zippy; both go well with appetizers. *Amontillado*, which is aged longer in the cask to become darker and richer, is also a bit sweeter with notes of hazelnut, and is typically served in between meals; sweet, acidic *oloroso* goes well with cheeses; the acid cuts through the fat. *Amontillado*, for one, is always fun to have on hand, especially at a large party. If you spot any old enemies—every honorable prep has at least one determined foe—hand them a glass and make a reference to that Poe story, especially if you're in a building where any noticeable renovations are going on. As always, understatement is key.

Ports of Call

When you come to think about it, sherry's cousin vintage port has more in common with Thunderbird (see Chapter 5, "Slummin' ") than one may first expect. Both are fortified wines—with nearly 20 percent alcohol volumes—that will knock the unsuspecting for a loop. Both are an acquired taste, to put it mildly. And both function as dessert for their respective connoisseurs. The main difference is one of price: a bottle of T-Bird sells for about $2; a vintage port can fetch $50 or more.

Like sherry, port hails from southern Europe; the name comes from Portugal, where the wines were first created. Nevertheless, ports have a heavily Anglo reputation, even more so than sherries. Churchill used to begin his day with a glass. The fact that with the exception of young ruby ports, the wines must be aged in order *to be* ports is another preppy feather in their cap. *Tawny ports*, for instance, are aged in wood for several years until they turn their signature tawny brown color. *Vintage ports* are kept in wood for two years and then aged in the bottle for years afterward; *late-bottle vintages* are kept in wood for a bit longer, usually around five years. In any case, the whole process requires lots of time: the best ports are aged for at least twenty years—which means that some of the finest ports these days come from the high-prep era.

Whites: As with Tennis,
As with Drinking

In the very early 1980s, "I'll just have a glass of white wine, please," became the mantra from Greenwich to Grosse Pointe, from Wellesley to Wheaton. The economy was in the doldrums, the old family industries were suffering, and the stock dividends were down. It was enough to drive one to drink—though, then again, it was never hard for preps to find excuses to drink. Still, a Reagan recession booze binge would mean putting on weight—a general prep no-no. *Voilà!* The dry white wine solution. It was light (eighty calories per glass); it projected an image of good sense (white wine had less alcohol than, say, an old-fashioned); it allowed for the exercise of one's long forgotten French skills; and best of all, it let one get tipsy after a vigorous lunchtime squash game, yet return to the office no worse for the wear. By 1980, in fact, white wine was the single most popular drink *in America*. Although the white wine craze led to a rash of magazine stories throughout the decade about the growing population of "wino-holics" it was good for brightening up a prep palate numbed for too long by juniper berries and Angostura bitters. Ultimately, though, it proved to be more a female affair than a male one; preppy men, alas, have always been suckers for the red, the oaked, and the astringent.

SOAVE

A tart, light, *dry* white—with a crispness much like fresh linen. Soave first gained preppy cred in the late-1970s for being cheap, plentiful, Italian, and tolerably easy to pronounce. There's little sweetness here, yet the overall effect recalls wild nights from junior year study-abroad in Florence, every preppy's favorite excuse for taking a yearlong academic vacation. Produced in the ancient walled town of the same name, Soave took off in a big way during the 1970s, when the Italian wine industry attempted to shed its low-rent, Chianti-bottle-wrapped-in-straw image and reach an international audience. One winery in particular, Bolla, marketed the hell out of Soave throughout the 1980s, so much so that many came to believe that Soave was a proprietary brand. Although Bolla grossly misunderstood Soave's true audience by comparing the wine with the gauche Memphis design that infected the '80s with a plague of tackiness, preppies rolled their eyes at such comparisons and kept on drinking. Soave was the favorite wine of Dante Aligheri.

FRASCATI

If you liked Ciardi's translation of *Inferno* during fifth-form World Literature, go with Soave; if you preferred the Walter Kaufmann translation of Goethe's *Faust*, however, go with the German wunderkind's favorite wine, Frascati. The archetypal light table wine, Frascati comes from Trebiano and Malvasia grapes grown in volcanic soil right outside of Rome. Although harder to find these days than it used to be, and although it has a reputation for not traveling well, it appeals to the same part of the preppy soul as Soave, except that Frascati is perhaps a little less dry; in that sense, consider Frascati the backyard badminton to the Soave clay-court tennis game.

CHABLIS

With Chablis, the distinction between the official European version and the everyday jug rendition comes to light.

The former *French* Chablis uses Pinot Chardonnay grapes and has a distinctly "flinty" taste with high acidity. Unlike run-of-the-mill Chardonnays (see page 138), these wines have some character. Good for a reserved gathering.

The latter *California* Chablis uses a mix of Chenin Blanc, Colombard, and Thompson Seedless grapes; it was favored by the likes of Erskine Caldwell and Donald Barthelme (ice cube optional). The wine came in quantity from Taylor and Paul Masson, though the paradigm for years was Gallo's Chablis Blanc, a blend that finally disappeared from American liquor store shelves in the 1990s. Thin, sweet, watery, with notes of vanilla, it's the sort of wine that snobs typically imagine elderly gentlemen in white ribbed turtlenecks, Kreskin-styled eyeglasses, and pinkie rings drinking on the veranda. But it's really not *that* bad. Its range is limited, true; yet so was Sinatra's. When needed in bulk, it does the trick.

RHINE

As with Chablis, both blended and original European versions are available; and as with Chablis, the two bear virtually no resemblance. California Rhine is a jug affair, though not necessarily to be scoffed at for that reason alone. Indeed, as sold by the likes of Gallo, the California Rhine is oft considered one of the main reasons for the growth of white wine at the end of the 1970s: it was bright, a dash sweet, yet reasonably low-cal. Such wines functioned as domestic interpretations of those wines produced from grapes grown near Germany's Rhine River. Although only grade-grind engineers and Henry Kissinger wannabes actually studied German in their prep years, the undeniable appeal of German beer lent the native Rhine wines a happy degree of preppiness, all things remaining equal.

The native Rhines—made from Riesling grapes—are not so much ickily, stickily saccharine as possessed of a kind of natural, springy, fruity sweetness. Rieslings range from moderately dry *Kabinetts*, to semisweet *Spätleses*, to very sweet *Ausleses* (which are often served as dessert wines). They are juicy, high in acid, mouthwatering; at their best, they have a tang akin to an early issue of *Spy Magazine*. Those inclined toward the German Rhines find them to fit like a springy pair of lime green Pappagallos, blossoms optional. Perfect for sipping at garden parties, they are also especially well suited for food, especially to dull preppy cuisine, which they lighten and to which they give sparkle. Although such *liebfraumilch* travesties as Blue Nun gave German wines a bad name during the high-prep era, such selections are not authentic Rhines. Rather, they were the plonk of choice for washed-up L.A. session musicians during the Carter years. Rieslings are the special prize for the prep who knows better: they're cheap, drinkable, and endlessly refreshing.

SAUVIGNON BLANC

The typical selection for preps who've maxed out on Soave, are looking for a new grape, and who deduce that Sauvignon Blanc might bear some kind of vague resemblance to the red Cabernet Sauvignon. Although both American and French versions use the same grape (namely, Sauvignon

Blanc), the wines differ fundamentally, as one might expect. The high acidity found in the grassy, pungent Gallic rendition makes the wine deliciously mouthwatering—and thus perfect for long parties and social events where one has to talk for hours.

When aged with oak, as is often the case with California versions, however, the wine is called Fumé Blanc—though unscrupulous American wineries may not make clear that their wines are so treated. Like a strenuous year of AP Calculus, the oak process zaps an otherwise good wine of character and wit. You'll know it when you taste it: If a restaurant slips you a Fumé, you may believe that your waiter has tried hoodwinking you with a glass of Chardonnay.

BUT WHAT ABOUT CHARDONNAY?

Jules (Demi Moore): "You could order a nice Napa Valley Chardonnay. Or if she's really worth it, you could get an import to impress her."
Kirby (Emilio Estevez): "Well, money's no object."
Jules: "Really? Then Montrachet or Meursault. And make sure you smell the cork."

—A PHONE EXCHANGE FROM *ST. ELMO'S FIRE* (1985)

So what *about* Chardonnay? Some people just *lurrrve* Chardonnay: generally, they talk about its "buttery simplicity" or its "delicious hints of oak." But despite popular stereotype, Chardonnay's definitely not for preps. Montrachet and Meursault are both highly respectable French varieties, if a little pricey and a little nouveau; but make sure you smell *the cork*? Oh, Demi. . . .

As the sage Willie Gluckstern, the self-styled "Wine Avenger," points out in his eponymous book, Chardonnay is basically flavorless white grape juice fermented in barrels filled with oak cubes. The result is a woody, and wooden, affair, a cause solely for 1980s Euro-poseurs and sun-wrinkled celebrity chefs who tried to con the rest of the world with self-justifying propaganda about California Destiny. Imagine drinking your old family dinner table and you'll understand the essence of Chardonnay. With respect to the zillion-dollar Napa Valley vintages that started popping up in the 1980s, Chardonnay was the kind of wine that unctuous plastic surgeons who collected Patrick Nagel prints were apt to ply on the unsuspecting in lame seduction schemes. (Yes, Demi?) "Chard" looks nice in a brand-new refrigerator, or perhaps even in a still life, but when a price tag comes attached, it's a case of the Emperor's New Gucci Clothes. And unfortunately, as a glance at the wine lists of any university clubhouse nowadays will confirm, the illusion has snared more than a few innocents. So the next time the catering staff at the art gallery opening tries to hit you with some, go for the bourbon or the Amstel Light or—anything else.

WATER INTO WINE

White wine kept off the pounds, but for those who liked things even lighter, there was the white wine spritzer. Just mix equal parts white wine and club soda in one wineglass. Serve on ice with a lemon twist.

Reds: No, Not the Three-Hour Warren Beatty Movie

During the 1980s, the love of red wine began for some preps at an early age. At many boarding schools affiliated with the Episcopal Church, students were expected to attend chapel service. While the 1970s brought to an end the practice of compulsory chapel service at most places, voluntary chapel service usually drew sparse crowds. The exception was Friday night communion, where the chaplain served the red wine; indeed, Friday night piety hour led students at some schools to take pride in consuming more wine than their peers at other institutions. Once again, such students showed the special prep knack for adhering nominally to rules in order to secretly undermine them. (A certain Andover grad did something like this in a recent presidential election.)

As the 1980s took hold, white wines outsold reds five to one in American bars. Partly, this was due to the popular belief that white were less likely to give you a pounding headache (not true); partly, it was due to the belief that most reds were not ideal cocktail drinks (true). Still, at the preppy garden party where the guys are sporting flipped-up IZODs *en masse*, the reds are bound to come out.

BEAUJOLAIS

If white wine were red, it would be Beaujolais—preppy red wine drinking at its best. It has everything right going for it. It's light, it's refreshing, it has body, and you can slug down a lot of it without getting too hammered. At midnight on the third Wednesday of November, the annual *Beaujolais*

Nouveau makes its debut: You have to drink it within a few months, but it's always a good sign that the autumn social season is back and kicking. Despite the name, it's thoroughly prep.

Other Beaujolais wines are released on December 15, and should not be drunk at least until summering season begins. The best are the *Beaujolais-Villages* wines, which come from the best Beaujolais growing regions in France; nevertheless, some decent non-Beaujolais-Villages wines are available. Like a good guest, Beaujolais does not outwear its welcome.

BURGUNDY

If your prep school library were a wine, it would be burgundy. Dark, full-bodied, and full of history, burgundy is produced from Pinot Noir grapes and is aimed at those with the wallets to buy it. In its Gallic rendition, the result is softer, fruitier, and smoother than the typical Bordeaux. In its Gallo rendition—typified by their "Hearty Burgundy"— the result is what one imagines as a sangria base for hippies. Yet once again, the overall concoction is not all that bad. Although not produced from Pinot Noir, the domestic blend is surprisingly drinkable: It's full-bodied with notes of berry and cherry, all sans oak and at a low price.

CABERNET SAUVIGNON

Like the stern headmaster who loves to convene meetings of the Disciplinary Committee, Cabernet Sauvignon is the gray eminence of red wines: preppy males, convinced that dry red wine is the only way to go, head for "Cab" by instinct. Like this crowd's thick leather briefcases, Cabernet

Sauvignon is high in tannins. The result is sometimes akin to said headmaster's infamous seminar on the Glorious Revolution of 1688, but not all Cabernets are equal. Bad Cabernet experiences are typically the results of preppies buying cheap Chilean bottles from the bargain bin at the Main Liquor Store in College Town; these wines are fine at staining one's pearly whites, yet they don't do much for the palate.

Other preps fare better (though at greater cost) with the French chateau varieties, a.k.a. *Bordeaux*, which are Cabernet Sauvignons smoothed out a dash with some merlot, and then left to age. In the process, the tannins mellow out and the result is a fine wine, though one that must be decanted. The issue of which vintage Bordeaux to pursue lies outside the purview of this book, of course, though Kingsley Amis has it right: "Vintages—aargh! Most of the crap talked about wine centres on these." Older is not necessarily better.

AND MERLOT?

This one hit big around the end of the 1980s and continues on strong today, as Cabernet overload prompted the wine corps to champion a new grape. Like that great pretender Chardonnay, Merlot is essentially like primer paint: with no real character on its own, it gains most of its flavor from oak. If you've tasted one, you've tasted them all. Often requested at university faculty parties by neo-conservative political theorists who look like Gene Shalit, but think they're English, the bludgeoning and overpriced Merlot is best avoided by any preppy who has better options. There are always better options.

Introducing Jack's Brother, Wine-in-a-Box

Wine-in-a-box, however, is not necessarily a better option. That peculiar invention of the 1980s, wine-in-a-box (or more properly, wine-in-a-bag-in-a-box), has a lot in common with 1980s pop music. In the music case, a synthesizer melody thumps along as an Eddie Van Halen-ish electric guitar lick plays over top. Although preps never really fell for the *Miami Vice* thing, wine-in-a-box has a similar spirit—it's something effete (i.e., wine) trying to masquerade itself in a tough (i.e., pseudo-keg) exterior. As with classic, pre–Lean Cuisine Stouffer dinners, all preps hated to admit they liked them, yet those bags-in-boxes sure seemed to come in *handy* somehow. . . .

Invented in 1982 by some fertile minds with a droll sense of humor, wine-in-a-box had all the virtues of its jug counterparts, except with a longer lasting life. Once opened, the Mr. Science–created bag kept the leftover wine fresh for six weeks; this made it easy for wine drunks to have some on hand in the refrigerator at any hour of the day or night. Introduced by Almaden, refined by Caraffa d'Oro, and pushed to the limits of good taste by Franzia, wine-in-a-box performed its low but solid duties at dorm basement parties, toga bacchanals, and hasty weekend Cape Cod barbecues through the end of the decade.

Boxed wines come in a spectrum of varieties, both varietals and blends. White Zinfandels and Chardonnays are easy enough to find, though boxed-wine producers are introducing more reds these days in a search to "tone up" their product. Prices range from about $8 for a three-liter box to about $13 for a five-liter box. A Faustian bargain, perhaps, but a bargain nonetheless.

Champagne and Sparkling Wine: The Preppy Dilemma

"Champagne. Perfume going in, sewage coming out."

—TOM CRUISE, *COCKTAIL* (1988)

And sometimes, even going in, it's not so wonderful. At its best, champagne—technically speaking, sparkling wine from a region of France approximately ninety miles northeast of Paris—*is* a wonder: upon first sip, the liquid transforms itself into millions of tiny bubbles, and the rush goes straight to one's head. The sad truth be told, however, preppies aren't particularly good with champagne and sparkling wines from other regions. When one realizes the vast range of good champagnes on the planet, the narrowed palate that automatically goes for the dry must be accepted with disappointment and loss. Attend enough preppy Christmas parties, and you're apt to find the same damned *brut* champagnes and sparkling wines over and over again. This is not to say that one must take up the lost '60s causes of Cold Duck, or—heaven forfend—Champale. Nevertheless, when confronted with the *brut* parade, one yearns for the *extra dry* (which is actually *less* dry than *brut*), the *sec* (which is typically sweet), and the *demi-sec*. Champagne should be about fun and frivolity, about joining Anita Ekberg in that walk through the fountain. Yet it's a sad fact: The typical preppy champagne or sparkling buyer is virtually *guaranteed* to head for one of the following.

MOËT & CHANDON WHITE STAR

Standard-issue respectable *brut* champagne. A perennial choice at winter balls throughout the land; especially popular among disco flunkies of Truman Capote. Preppy common sense understands it to be the be-all, end-all for most practical purposes; yet when one drinks it, the words of the late Miss Peggy Lee come to mind: "Is that all there *is?*"

CORDON NEGRO

A cheaper Spanish sparkling wine, produced by Freixenet and aged in a cave for three years; thus, C.N. is known as a "cava" wine. The only reasons anyone buys it are the enigmatic black bottles and the urban legend that it tastes good. Usually served as an aperitif, Cordon Negro also shows up as the refreshment of choice at "Gatsby" parties, wherein well-heeled preps rent off-season Cape Cod mansions while pretending to be proles pretending to be well-heeled.

HERE'S CORK IN YOUR EYE

The typical bottle of champagne has *three times* the air pressure of the average car tire. So unless you want to give dear Bitsy a concussion with a jet-propelled stray cork, here's how to open a champagne bottle with safety and aplomb.

1. Remove the metal foil and wire cage around the cork, but keep your thumb on top of the cork to keep it safely in place.

2. Take the bottle in your left hand and wrap your right hand around the neck, with your thumb and forefinger around the cork. Make sure the bottle's not pointing at any of your friends.

3. Tilt the bottle to about 45 degrees. Holding the cork, delicately twist the bottle, but don't remove the cork all the way.

4. Once you feel confident that the cork is in your control, remove it.

Tilting the bottle allows air to fill the neck, thus preventing the champagne from gushing out. And that's important: The less gas that escapes from the bottle, the less flat and more vivacious the champagne will be.

NOTE: Whatever you do, *never* put a champagne bottle into a freezer. Otherwise, you'll hear the muffled "pop" of the exploding glass within about twenty minutes.

A "Méthode Champenois" sparkling wine from Sonoma, California. (That is, although not a true champagne—which would have to come from the Champagne region of France—it uses the same fermentation methods that the French wines use.) The official sparkling wine of the Kennedy Administration, you're apt to have found this at the last several presidential inaugural parties and at countless preppy weddings. It's cheaper than White Star, yet not so cheap as to fall into André territory.

One might be surprised not to find White Star's upscale brother, Dom Perignon, on the list. Alas, while certain European types may go for this, preps find it hard to imagine shelling out the big bucks for a bottle of champagne. It's like Shakespeare: Everyone praises it, but few drink it. Much better to go for a decent single malt at half the price—or to stock an *entire bar* for even less—than to lose one's money over something so ephemeral and bubbly as champagne.

The Wall of Shame

THE WAGES OF ZIN: PINK, BUT NOT PRETTY

In the early '80s, American wine growers faced an overproduction of Zinfandel grapes. What to do? Turn 'em into pop wine! The result was the decade's super-seller, White Zinfandel, which was lighter than a rosé and sweeter than a box of raisins. While dyed-in-the-cask preps eventually took to Chardonnay and Merlot, White Zinfandel was strictly verboten.

Taking the Waters:
Aqueous Alternatives

"What do people who don't drink have? Ginger ale, ice water . . . ? I don't know. Maybe a Coke—with an aspirin."

—FRED (BRYAN LEDER), *METROPOLITAN* (1990)

Maybe it has something to do with prep love for all things nautical, but in the 1980s, water found its own place in the prep bar. As comic sociologist Paul Fussell has made clear, water sends an important message: "I used to drink heavily, and thus formerly was funny, careless, adventuresome, etc. [but] I had the sense to give it up, and am thus both intelligent and disciplined." Preps wanted to be both intelligent and disciplined—or at least perceived as such. And, frankly, sometimes it's hard to be either when you're drinking.

In the early 1980s, we weren't deluged with hundreds of brands of bottled water, sparkling and seltzer water, juice, and iced tea all competing for our thirst. The top five drinks at the time were all soft drinks: Coke, Pepsi, Dr Pepper, 7-Up, and TaB. The average American obviously had a congenital weakness for syrupy sweetness. Preppies, however, did not and were the first to trumpet the cause of bottled water. Although the prospect of paying money for something you could get free from the tap struck the stodgier prep as an imminent sign of decadence, there was no turning back the tide. Eighties consumers were in fact ready and willing to pay for water bottled at the source or otherwise. In 1980, bottled water sales were double what they had been just four years earlier, which made bottled water the fastest growing drink around. Dentists even began to see an increase in cavities in their patients who had switched from fluoridated tap water to bottled.

Sales of diet soft drinks also exploded in the '80s. While preppies, largely suspicious of the fake sweeteners, embraced diet soda even less than they embraced regular soda, some prep women were swayed by the matriarch of the genre, TaB. (See Chapter 4, "Come Out Swinging.") As with Virginia Slims cigarettes, there was never any question about TaB's target market. (The more gender-neutral diet Coke was not yet the standard breakfast drink among publicists and models it would become later in the decade.)

In 1985, the Coca-Cola Company attempted to ride the yuppie wave by introducing New Coke. The public re-volted and the "original" Coke returned with a new name: Coca-Cola Classic. Soft drinks may not be preppy, but Clas-sic Coke clearly wins the Preppy Challenge against upstart Pepsi—even if traditionalists were hoping for a revival of Coke's *real* original recipe.

So what did the health-conscious or liver-weakened prep drink?

Perrier: The *Other* Greenie

Since green is one of the most important colors in the preppy wardrobe, it follows that the prep has a natural affin-ity for the green-bottled Perrier. Technically "mineral" wa-ter, Perrier has been bottled only at the source in Vergeze, France, since 1863 and was introduced in the United States in the late 1970s. Perfect timing. To stay sane during the disco era preps *had* to drink. By the last days of disco their habits had caught up with them.

Credited with beginning the bottled water revolution in this country, Perrier also appealed to health-conscious yuppies. While yupsters enjoyed it for its trendy Euro-value and series of collectible "art" bottles, preppies liked the taste and appreciated that if you take away one R and add two P's you get PREPPIER! Both Baby Boomer preps and yups were becoming aware of their mortality for the first time and Perrier targeted them with an "Enjoy It in Good Health" advertising campaign. It worked. For the first time, sparkling water "instead of a cocktail" actually seemed like a good idea. Add a lime and with the bubbles it's *almost* a real drink. At least it looks like a G&T.

Preps, immortal and always in good health, chose bottled water for another reason: decorum. Almost every prep drinker knows when to say when. Or Uncle.

> ACCESSORY: *A pipe (The best way to avoid being perceived as too "California")*
> ACTIVITY: *Tennis*
> DON'T: *Drink from the bottle. Pour it into a glass. Unlike yuppies, preps don't advertise—for free.*

Saratoga Water: Miss Preppy

Preppier and more exclusive than Perrier, Saratoga Water has been bottled at the source, Sweet Water Spring in Saratoga Springs, New York, since 1872. Back in the day, celebrities drank America's first bottled water from monogrammed cups.

Located at the foothills of the Adirondacks, Saratoga Springs has been a summering choice for thoroughbred New Yorkers since the early 19th century, when word of the local waters' curative powers spread down the Eastern Seaboard. It's also the home of the country's oldest race-track, as well as Skidmore College and Yaddo, one of the nation's oldest artist and writer's retreats. (Although we suspect that the participants indulge in more than just the local waters.) Polo returned to Saratoga Springs in the 1970s after a hiatus of nearly four decades, by the early 1980s, the town was galloping.

ACCESSORY: *Summer hat*
ACTIVITY: *Taking the waters*
DON'T: *Loan out your binoculars*

Tonic Water: Go Native

That's right. When you need a little more than Saratoga Water has to offer, and when maybe gin is no longer a choice, there's only one option here: Schweppes, the British bubbly. Who else but the Brits know how to make tonic right? Dating from the early days of the British Empire, tonic water contains quinine and thus was used to ward off malaria in India. In fact, it is actually known as Indian Tonic Water in many countries, though not in the politically correct United States. Although Joseph Conrad is a popular summer reading author, preps don't like to be reminded of their colonial past.

Serve it straight, over ice, in an old-fashioned glass with a slice of lime. Ignore others' disbelief that you're actually drinking tonic water straight. Sit back and enjoy the quinine's muscle relaxant properties.

ACCESSORY: *Mosquito netting*
ACTIVITY: *Business lunch*
DON'T: *Fake a British accent*

NOTE: For those unwilling to take their tonic water straight, there's always Bitter Lemon, a British favorite, which has all the quinine, but with an added citrus zing.

"Physical Education courses are tennis, hockey, lacrosse, basketball, volleyball, soccer, rhythms, folk dancing, tumbling, calisthenics, apparatus work, gymnastics, and badminton."—THE SHIPLEY SCHOOL, BRYN MAWR, PENNSYLVANIA

Seltzer Water: Pump It Up

Of course, Perrier isn't necessarily available at every bar. And straight tonic water is a bit intense for those of us who come into contact only with Cape Cod mosquitoes. In that case, opt for generic seltzer water. Seltzer water is just carbonated water. Unlike club soda, which has mineral salts, seltzer has no sodium and no calories. (Club soda, however, removes troublesome red wine stains.) Both are considered soft drinks, as opposed to Perrier, which is considered sparkling water because its carbonation is its natural level. Jean Jacob Schweppe first carbonated water in a Swiss lab in the 1780s. In the 1980s urban preps loved their seltzer and made it themselves at home with classic crystal siphons or received a visit from the seltzer man.

ACCESSORY: *"The Journal"*
ACTIVITY: *Air travel*
DON'T: *Drink the fruit-flavored varieties*

Wall of Shame

WHAT DOES *EVIAN* SPELL BACKWARDS?

Eighties models subsisted on the big liter bottles of this spring water from the French Alps—which led to the invention of that stupid water bottle-holding bag used only by models. If only their lifestyles were so wholesome.

"Not to be served, but to serve."

—MOTTO OF THE TAFT SCHOOL, WATERTOWN, CONNECTICUT

Social Calendar:
A Year of Prepping Dangerously

J. D. Salinger's Birthday	January 1
James Spader's Birthday	February 7
Valentine's Day	February 14
St. Patrick's Day	March 17
Phillips Exeter Academy founded	April 3, 1781
F. Scott Fitzgerald and Zelda Sayre's Anniversary	April 3, 1920
Henry Sands Brooks opens H. & D. H. Brooks in New York City	April 7, 1918
Tax Day	April 15
May Day	May 1

Kentucky Derby	First Saturday in May
Cinco de Mayo	May 5
Mare Winningham's Birthday	May 16, 1959
Memorial Day; Summering season begins	Last Monday in May
John Cheever dies in Ossining, New York	June 19, 1982
Block Island Race Week	Last Week of June, biannually; first held in 1965
John McEnroe (Trinity School '77) defeats Bjorn Borg at Wimbledon	July 4, 1981
Bastille Day	July 14
Congress passes the National Minimum Drinking Age Act, increasing the national drinking age to 21	July 17, 1984
Labor Day	First Monday in September
Black Monday; J. Peterman founds clothing company	October 7, 1987
Head of the Charles	Third Saturday and Sunday in October; first held October 16, 1965
Halloween	October 31
Homecoming Weekend	October/November

"The Game" (Harvard vs. Yale)	Mid-November
Prohibition repealed	December 5, 1933
New Year's Eve	December 31

To the Betamax:
Preppy Movies to Drink By

After Hours (1985)

Directed by Martin Scorsese. Starring Griffin Dunne, Rosanna Arquette, John Heard, Teri Garr, Cheech and Chong.

The classic slummin' nightmare: Dominick Dunne's son cabs it to SoHo one night, loses his money, and fights for survival against a vigilante mob of trendy artists.

Animal House (1978)

Directed by John Landis. Starring John Belushi, Tim Matheson, Donald Sutherland.

Since 1978, students at every preppy college in the United States have insisted that *their* campus's resident stoner professor was in fact the inspiration for the Donald Sutherland character.

Barcelona **(1994)**

Directed by Whit Stillman. Starring Taylor Nichols, Christopher Eigeman, and Mira Sorvino.

American preppies in Barcelona read Peter Drucker, dodge anti-American terrorists, and fall in love.

Caddyshack **(1980)**

Directed by Harold Ramis. Starring Chevy Chase, Rodney Dangerfield, Ted Knight, and Bill Murray.

Slobs versus snobs versus gophers at the local country club. Be the ball.

Caligula **(1980)**

Directed by Tinto Brass (with "additional footage" by Bob Guccione). Starring Malcolm McDowell, Sir John Gielgud, Peter O'Toole, and Helen Mirren.

Penthouse publisher Guccione, a Blair Academy grad, revisits his toga party days with this X-rated romp "adapted from an original screenplay" by preppy eminence Gore Vidal. Slummin' members of the British acting gentry stumble through expensive sets during orgy scenes. Gore sued to have his name removed from the credits; he later resurfaced with Charlie Sheen and Linda Hamilton in *The Shadow Conspiracy* (1997).

Carnal Knowledge **(1971)**

Directed by Mike Nichols. Starring Jack Nicholson, Art Garfunkel, Ann-Margret, and Candice Bergen.

Bleak portrait of Amherst-Smith mixer scene and life thereafter.

Class (1983)

Directed by Lewis John Carlino. Starring Rob Lowe, Jacqueline Bisset, and Andrew McCarthy.

Skip (Lowe) is a prep school senior. Jonathan (McCarthy) is his new roommate. Although he looks about twelve, Jonathan soon meets Skip's mother (Bisset) at a Chicago bar, convinces her he's a Northwestern grad student, and carries on an affair with her. Inevitably, Mom discovers Jonathan's identity while on a shopping spree in a New York Burberry's. (Don't leave your student ID in your tweed jacket pockets, boys!) Jonathan doesn't discover Mom's identity, however, until he arrives home to spend the holidays at Skip's estate. After duking it out in the mud, both boys get into Harvard; it's going to be okay. Filmed at Lake Forest College.

Cocktail (1988)

Directed by Roger Donaldson. Starring Tom Cruise, Bryan Brown, and Elisabeth Shue.

An honest lad with a burning dream shows up in New York City, mixes some drinks, recites some "poetry," and finds true love. Cruise reportedly did all his own bottle-tossing.

Endless Love (1981)

Directed by Franco Zeffirelli. Starring Brooke Shields, Martin Hewitt, and James Spader.

Shields's faux-liberal parents—egged on by petulant, skeet-shooting older brother Spader—stop creepy Hewitt from dating her. In response, Hewitt burns their house down to Blondie's "Heart of Glass." Upon release from the asylum, Hewitt pops up in New York City, where Brooke's mother hits on him at Pete's Tavern. Spader made this a few years after dropping out of Andover. Tom Cruise's first film.

Friday the 13th (1980)

Directed by Sean Cunningham. Starring Betsy Palmer, Adrienne King, and Harry Crosby.

Culver Academy and Yale grad Gene Siskel tried to convince viewers of *Sneak Previews* to write letters to Betsy Palmer to express their outrage at her showing up in such trash. Siskel later ended up buying John Travolta's white disco suit at auction.

Friday the 13th Part 2 (1981)

Directed by Steve Miner. Starring Amy Steel, John Furey, and Warrington Gillette.

More preppy mayhem at Camp Crystal Lake. Sample romantic dialogue:

Man: "Football and hockey. Which do you prefer?"
Woman: "The one with the puck."

Igby Goes Down (2002)

Directed by Burr Steers. Starring Kieran Culkin, Ryan Phillipe, Amanda Peet, and Claire Danes.

Preppies gone wild, but with a name like "Igby," what other choice do you have? Well-connected director Steers played the deep-voiced doorman Van in *The Last Days of Disco;* he's also the nephew of Gore Vidal and Jackie Kennedy *and* the cousin of Louis Auchincloss.

The Last Days of Disco (1998)

Directed by Whit Stillman. Starring Chloe Sevigny, Kate Beckinsale, Christopher Eigeman, Matt Keeslar, Mackenzie Astin.

Have you ever seen such preppy Hampshire grads? Dancing, romancing, and book publishing in very early '80s Manhattan. The Old Town Bar makes a cameo.

Legally Blonde (2001)
Directed by Robert Luketic. Starring Reese Witherspoon, Luke Wilson, and Selma Blair.

The preppy returns as B-movie stock villain in this harmless comedy set at Harvard Law School. *Felicity* meets *Pretty Woman* meets *The Paper Chase* meets *Erin Brockovich*. See *Election* instead.

Love Story (1970)
Directed by Arthur Hiller. Starring Ryan O'Neal and Ali MacGraw.

Tragic preppy romance, as produced by the inimitable Robert "The Kid" Evans. Sequel *Oliver's Story* (1978) starred O'Neal, but obviously not MacGraw.

Making the Grade (1984)
Directed by Dorian Walker. Starring Judd Nelson, Jonna Lee, and Dana Olsen.

In real life, Judd Nelson went to St. Paul's and studied philosophy for two years at Haverford. Here, he plays a street punk who impersonates a spoiled preppy who's spending his senior year fooling around in Europe. A young Andrew Clay plays a bookie named "Dice"; everyone wears yellow and pink. From the producers of *The Delta Force* and *Death Wish III*.

Metropolitan (1990)
Directed by Whit Stillman. Starring Carolyn Farina, Edward Clements, Christopher Eigeman.

Boy from the wrong side of the Park becomes a member of the Sally Fowler Rat Pack during the Christmas debutante season. The first in Whit Stillman's preppy trilogy; see also *Barcelona* and *The Last Days of Disco*. Essential viewing all.

Ordinary People (1980)
Directed by Robert Redford. Starring Donald Sutherland, Mary Tyler Moore, and Timothy Hutton.

Teenage Suicide—Don't Do It. Partially filmed at Lake Forest College.

Oxford Blues (1984)
Directed by Robert Boris. Starring Rob Lowe, Ally Sheedy, Amanda Pays, and Julian Firth.

Las Vegas parking valet and all-around pretty boy Rob Lowe indulges Anglo nobility stalker fantasies at Oxford. He wards off potential male suitors from the rowing team by pursuing torrid affair with fellow American Ally Sheedy. Filmed in '38 as *A Yank at Oxford*.

The Preppie Murder (1989)
Directed by John Herzfeld. Starring Danny Aiello, William Baldwin, and Lara Flynn Boyle.

The movie-of-the-week version, introducing Sandra Bullock in a bit part and starring William Baldwin as Robert Chambers. 'Nuff said.

Preppies (1982)
Directed by Chuck Vincent. Starring Dennis Drake, Steven Holt, and Katt Shea.

Early-'80s preppy life as hallucinated by an ex–porn director with financing from Hef's Playboy Channel. Chip has to pass his econ final or else his trust fund will go to his evil cousin. Said evil cousin hires some vixens to distract Chip and usurp his fortune. On the theatrical release poster, an IZOD-clad prep totes a Thompson submachine gun.

Preppy School Girls (1978) (a.k.a. Boarding School; Virgin Campus; Leidenschaftliche Blümchen)

Directed by Andre Farwagi. Starring Nastassja Kinski and Gerry Sundquist.

Eurosleaze set in a secluded West German girls' school. With the early star turn from Kinski, you probably can fill in the rest. Available on DVD for $5.99. Don't say we didn't warn you.

Prep School (1981)

Directed by Paul Almond. Starring Leslie Hope, Andrew Sabiston, and Gavin Brannan.

Preppies Chip and Drifty try to bring down the steely housemaster Arthur "Sherlock" Holmes at their New England boarding school. You can't help thinking there's something a wee bit strange aboot these preppies, when it suddenly all becomes clear: they're actually a bunch of bloody Canadians!

Pretty in Pink (1986)

Directed by John Hughes. Starring Molly Ringwald, Andrew McCarthy, Jon Cryer, and James Spader.

Isn't she? The car, the dress, the sound track, Iona, Duckie's lip synch to "Try a Little Tenderness." Good times. Watching it now, it's obvious redheads shouldn't wear pink, Blaine was gay, and Andie should have gone to prom with Duckie. But we didn't know that then.

Private School (for Girls) (1983)

Directed by Noel Black. Starring Matthew Modine, Phoebe Cates, and Betsy Russell.

Basically a movie-length episode of *Bosom Buddies*—only with Matthew Modine and real bosoms. Sylvia Kristel, who starred as the family maid in semi-prequel *Private Lessons* (1981), has a cameo as the headmistress.

Risky Business (1983)

Directed by Paul Brickman. Starring Tom Cruise, Rebecca DeMornay, Joe Pantoliano.

Suburban Chicago teenager Joel Goodson (Cruise) wants to major in business at Princeton. Unaware that Princeton doesn't actually offer a business major, however, he ends up a flesh merchant. "Porsche. There is no substitute."

Six Degrees of Separation (1993)

Directed by Fred Schepisi. Starring Stockard Channing, Will Smith, and Donald Sutherland.

Never give away your children's pink shirts. Based on the John Guare play, which was based on a real incident, not Kevin Bacon.

St. Elmo's Fire (1985)

Directed by Joel Schumacher. Starring The Brat Pack (Emilio Estevez, Rob Lowe, Andrew McCarthy, Demi Moore, Judd Nelson, Ally Sheedy, and Mare Winningham).

Seven Georgetown grads adjust to life in the "real world." The high-prep era comes to an end—as does the Brat Pack.

Tadpole (2002)

Directed by Gary Winick. Starring Sigourney Weaver, John Ritter, Bebe Neuwirth, and Aaron Stanford.

Neuwirth gets it on with male boarding school jailbait. But he has the eye for Ethel Walker grad Weaver. Add Ritter to the mix and four's a crowd.

Toy Soldiers (1991)

Directed by Daniel Petrie Jr. Starring Sean Astin, Wil Wheaton, Denholm Elliot, and Louis Gossett Jr.

Although it came out in the early '90s, it was based on a 1988 William P. Kennedy novel. It's *Class* meets *Rambo* as crafty prepsters outwit the Columbian narcoterrorists holding their Virginia boarding school hostage.

Trading Places (1983)

Directed by John Landis. Starring Dan Ackroyd, Eddie Murphy, and Jamie Lee Curtis.

Philadelphia gentleman Ackroyd swaps lives with con artist Murphy. The first major American film to explore the machinations of the pork commodities market.

Valley Girl (1983)

Directed by Martha Coolidge. Starring Deborah Foreman and Nicolas Cage.

"Tommy's got the bod, but his brain is bad news." Although no preppy in the history of the world has ever stepped foot in the grody San Fernando Valley, the movie is, like, filled to the max with awesome flipped-up Lacostes.

The World According to Garp (1981)

Directed by George Roy Hill. Starring Robin Williams, Glenn Close, John Lithgow, and Mary Beth Hurt.

Williams trades in rainbow suspenders for preppy sweaters in the film adaptation of Exeter wrestling champion John Irving's novel. Coincidentally, he and Lithgow both would play TV aliens. A summertime hit at Cape Cod's Wellfleet Drive-In Theater.

APPENDIX C

Elective Summer Reading:
Preps Read Bestsellers, Too

Popular preppy picks from the *Publishers Weekly* bestseller list (with years noted).

1. *Oliver's Story*, Erich Segal ('77)
   Yale Classics tenure casualty laughs en route to bank with *Love Story* sequel.

2. *Mommie Dearest*, Christina Crawford ('78)
   Starch and box.

3. *Cruel Shoes*, Steve Martin ('79)
   Weejuns, loafers, Top-Siders, wing tips.

4. *The Complete Scarsdale Medical Diet*, Dr. Herman Tarnower, M.D., and Samm Sinclair Baker ('79)

The original preppy murder case: Madeira School headmistress Jean Harris was convicted of shooting Tarnower, her boyfriend.

5. *The Hotel New Hampshire*, John Irving ('81)
   Such a lovely place, such a lovely face.

6. *Cujo*, Stephen King ('81)
   When pets go bad, New England style.

7. *Miss Piggy's Guide to Life*, Miss Piggy as told to Henry Beard ('81)
   When farm animals go bad, Hollywood style.

8. *Jane Fonda's Workout Book*, Jane Fonda ('82)
   Emma Willard grad/Barbarella/Hanoi Jane/ Oscar winner/The future Mrs. Ted Turner gets physical.

9. *Hollywood Wives*, Jackie Collins ('83)
   Steamy shopping scenes.

10. *Return of the Jedi Storybook*, Joan D. Vinge, adapt. ('83)
    "Ewok"? That was my summer camp!

Gator!: Preppy Jukebox, c. 1980 (for Formal and Slummin' Occasions)

"God Only Knows"   The Beach Boys

"Eleanor Rigby"   The Beatles

"Heart of Glass"   Blondie

"Paper Moon"   Nat King Cole

"Working in the Coal Mine"   Lee Dorsey

"The Lady Is a Tramp"   Ella Fitzgerald

"Truckin' "   The Grateful Dead

"Don't Leave Me This Way"   Thelma Houston

"Shout"   The Isley Brothers

"I Want You Back"   The Jackson Five

"Piano Man"   Billy Joel

"Will You Love Me Tomorrow?"   Carole King

"Louie, Louie"	The Kingsmen
"California Dreamin' "	The Mamas and the Papas
"Boy from New York City"	Manhattan Transfer
"Could You Be Loved"	Bob Marley and the Wailers
"Don't Sit Under the Apple Tree (With Anyone Else But Me)"	The Glenn Miller Orchestra
"The Joker"	The Steve Miller Band
"Brown-Eyed Girl"	Van Morrison
"Message in a Bottle"	The Police
"I've Got You Under My Skin"	Cole Porter
"Try a Little Tenderness"	Otis Redding
"Unchained Melody"	The Righteous Brothers
"Miss You"	The Rolling Stones
"Upside Down"	Diana Ross
"You're So Vain"	Carly Simon
"Scarborough Fair"	Simon and Garfunkel
"It Was a Very Good Year"	Frank Sinatra
"I've Been Workin' My Way Back to You, Babe"	The Spinners
"My Old School"	Steely Dan
"Last Dance"	Donna Summer
"Psycho Killer"	Talking Heads

"Boogie Oogie Oogie" A Taste of Honey

"My Girl" The Temptations

"The Lion Sleeps Tonight" The Tokens

"Pressure Drop" Toots and the Maytals

"Sir Duke" Stevie Wonder

Mail Order:
Preppy Drinking Suppliers

College and University Bookstores

Amherst College: A.J. Hastings, 45 South Pleasant Street, Amherst, Mass. 01002. www.ajhastings.com.

Babson College: Babson College Bookstore, Reynolds Campus Center, Babson Park, Mass. 02457. http://babson.bkstore.com.

Bates College: Bates Bookstore, Lewiston, Maine 04240. www.bates.edu/bookstore.xml.

Bowdoin College: Bowdoin Bookstore, Smith Union, Brunswick, Maine 04011. www.bowdoin.edu/book store.

Colby College: Colby Bookstore, Roberts Union, 5400 Mayflower Hill, Waterville, Maine 04901. http://store513.collegestoreonline.com.

Colorado College: Colorado College Bookstore, 902 No. Cascade Avenue, Colorado Springs, Colo. 80946. www.coloradocollegebooks.com.

Connecticut College: Connecticut College Bookstore, College Center, Mohegan Avenue, New London, Conn. 06320. www.conncoll.bkstr.com.

Dartmouth College: 27 S. Main Street, Hanover, N.H. 03755. www.dartmouthcoop.com.

Denison University: Denison Bookstore, Slayter Hall, Granville, Ohio, 43023. www.denisonbookstore.com.

Georgetown University: Georgetown University Bookstore, 3800 Reservoir Rd. NW, Washington, D.C. 20057. www.georgetown.bkstr.com.

Hamilton College: Hamilton College Bookstore, 198 College Hill Road, Clinton, N.Y. 13323. www.bkstore.com/hamilton.

Harvard University: Harvard University Coop, 1400 Massachusetts Avenue, Cambridge, Mass. 02238. www.thecoop.com.

Hollins University (**neé College**): Hollins University Bookshop, 8004 Fishbur Drive, Roanoke, Va. 24020. http://shop.efollett.com/htmlroot/storehome/hollinsuniversity309.html.

Lake Forest College: Lake Forest College Bookstore, Lake Forest, Ill. 60045. http://shop.efollett.com/htmlroot/storehome/lakeforestcollege148.html.

Middlebury College: The College Store at Middlebury, 58 Hepburn Road, Middlebury, Vt. 05753. www.middlebury.edu/~store.

Princeton University: Princeton University Store, 36 University Place, Princeton, N.J. 08540. www.pustore.com.

Smith College: Grécourt Bookstore, 100 Green Street, Northampton, Mass. 01060. www.smith-estore.com.

St. Lawrence University: Brewer Bookstore, Brewer Field House, Canton, N.Y. 13617. www.brewerbookstore. com.

Sweet Briar College: The Book Shop, Sweet Briar, Va. 24595. www.bookshop.sbc.edu.

Trinity College: Trinity College Bookstore, 300 Summit Street, Mather Hall, Hartford, Conn. 06106. http:// trinity.bkstore.com.

University of Virginia: University of Virginia Bookstore, 400 Emmett Street, Charlottesville, Va. 22904. http:// www.bookstore.virginia.edu.

Vassar College: Vassar College Bookstore, Vassar College Campus Center, 124 Raymond Avenue, Poughkeepsie, N.Y. 12604. http://vassar.bkstore.com.

Washington and Lee University: Washington and Lee University Bookstore, Lexington, Va. 24450. http:// bookstore.wlu.edu.

Wellesley College: Wellesley College Campus Store, Clapp Library, 106 Central Street, Wellesley, Mass. 02481. http://shop.efollett.com/htmlroot/storehome/wellesley college534.html.

Wheaton College: Old Town Bookstore, 100 Tauton Avenue, Norton, Mass. 02766. http://shop.efollett.com/ htmlroot/storehome/wheatoncollege525.html.

Williams College: Williams Shop, 15 Spring Street, Williamstown, Mass. 01267. www.williams-shop.com.

Yale University: Yale Bookstore, 77 Broadway, New Haven, Conn. 06511. www.yalebookstore.com.

Vintage Items

The Brimfield Antiques Show, the largest outdoor antiques show in the world, is a swell place to search out vintage drinking ware. The show, which takes place on a stretch of Route 60 in tiny Brimfield, Massachusetts, three times a year, actually consists of nearly two dozen different markets run by individual promoters. The Town of Brimfield is responsible for setting the show's dates, which hover around Memorial Day, the Fourth of July, and Labor Day. Some of the bigger markets include:

- Dealer's Choice (508) 347-3929
- Heart-o-the-Mart (413) 245-9556
- J & J Promotions (413) 245-3436; www.jandj-brimfield.com
- Mays Antique Show (413) 245-9271; www.mays-brimfield.com

The show itself runs for five days at a time, with different fields opening different days. No matter what markets are open, however, you certainly won't be at a loss for things to look at.

Another excellent place to search out collectible cocktail shakers, vintage IZOD, and sundry other preppery is the Triple Pier Expo in Manhattan. The show is held twice a year (one weekend in March, two consecutive weekends in November) at Passenger Pier Terminals 88, 90, and 92 along the Hudson River. Check out www.stellashows.com for more information.

Websites

Alligator shirts: www.lacoste.com

Badminton set: www.eddiebauer.com

Bazzini nuts: www.restorationhardware.com

Bermuda shorts: www.triminghams.com

Chinos: www.jcrew.com

Club ties: www.jpressonline.com/home

Cocktail shakers: www.crateandbarrel.com

Dress shirts: www.brooksbrothers.com

Fair Isle sweaters: www.landsend.com

Flasks: www.natsherman.com

Golf knickers: www.pazzogolf.com

Hammocks: www.vermontcountrystore.com

Handsewn Camp Mocs: www.llbean.com

Madras: www.orvis.com

Nantucket Reds: www.nantucketreds.com

Pearls: www.talbots.com

Prep Porn: www.abercrombie.com

Resort Wear: www.lillypulitzer.com

Seersucker: www.cablecarclothiers.com

TaB: www.easycoffee.com/tabmaxor3cas.html

SELECTED BIBLIOGRAPHY

Amis, Kingsley. *On Drink*. New York: Harcourt, Brace, Jovanovich, 1973.

Arneson, D. J. *The Original Preppy Cookbook*. New York: Dell, 1981.

————. *The Original Preppy Jokebook*. New York: Dell, 1981.

Austin, Stephanie. *The Preppy Problem*. New York: Fawcett Juniper, 1984.

Baltzell, E. Digby. *Philadelphia Gentlemen: The Making of a National Upper Class*. New York: The Free Press, 1958.

————. *The Protestant Establishment: Aristocracy and Caste in America*. New York: Vintage Books, 1964.

Barrett, Joan and Sally F. Goldfarb. *The Insider's Guide to Prep Schools, 1979–1980 ed*. New York: Thomas Congdon Books/Dutton, 1979.

Birnbach, Lisa. *Lisa Birnbach's College Book*. New York: Villard Books, 1984.

Birnbach, Lisa, ed. *The Official Preppy Handbook*. New York: Workman, 1980.

Cheever, John. *The Stories of John Cheever*. New York: Ballantine, 1980.

Cookson, Peter W. and Caroline Hodges Persell. *Preparing for Power: America's Elite Boarding Schools*. New York: Basic Books, 1985.

Dillard, Annie. *An American Childhood*. New York: Harper & Row, 1987.

Duffy, Brian Ross. *The Poor Boy's Guide to Marrying a Rich Girl*. New York: Penguin Books, 1987.

Edmunds, Lowell. *Martini, Straight Up: The Classic American Cocktail*. Baltimore and London: The Johns Hopkins University Press, 1981, 1998.

Ellis, Bret Easton. *American Psycho*. New York: Vintage Books, 1990.

———. *Less Than Zero*. New York: Simon & Schuster, 1985.

Fitzgerald, F. Scott. *Babylon Revisited and Other Stories*. New York: Charles Scribner's Sons, 1960.

Flippin, Royce and Douglas McGrath. *Save An Alligator, Shoot a Preppie*. New York: A&W Visual Library, 1981.

Fussell, Paul. *Class: A Guide Through the American Status System*. New York: Touchstone Books, 1983.

Gluckstern, Willie. *The Wine Avenger*. New York: Fireside Books, 1998.

The Handbook of Private Schools: An Annual Descriptive Survey of Independent Education, 63rd ed. Boston: Porter Sargent Publishers, 1982.

Lanza, Joseph. *The Cocktail: The Influence of Spirits on the American Psyche*. New York: St. Martin's Press, 1995.

Parker, Robert B. *Ceremony: A Spenser Novel*. New York: Delacorte Press, 1982.

Rosso, Julee and Sheila Lukins, with Michael McLaughlin. *The Silver Palate Cookbook*. New York: Workman, 1982.

Schoenstein, Ralph. *The I-Hate-Preppies Handbook*. New York: Simon & Schuster, 1981.

Shields, Brooke. *On Your Own*. New York: Villard Books, 1985.

Stillman, Whit. *The Last Days of Disco, With Cocktails at Pertrossian Afterwards*. New York: Farrar, Straus, and Giroux, 2000.

ACKNOWLEDGMENTS

We wish to thank all the family members and friends who offered advice and encouragement as we worked on this book. The next round's on us. Four people to whom we're especially indebted for their helpful reflections and conversations are John R. W. Rudolph, who keeps the spirit of preppy drinking alive; walking anachronism Jonathon Keats; and Helen and Ernest "Dutchy" Smith Sr., who were eager to rid their cellar of the 1980s. Gerd Groenewold provided a timely translation. We're also grateful to our agent, Elizabeth Kaplan, and our editor, Sheila Curry Oakes. And we thank you for your support.

INDEX

MATT "JOHNNIE" WALKER prepared in the 1980s at Shady Side Academy in the Pittsburgh suburb of Fox Chapel. Although many have confused Shady Side with a retirement home, he eventually went on to graduate from Amherst College. A former contributing editor for *Soma*, he worked for several years as an editor at a New York publishing house. Today, he continues his firsthand research into the prep universe as a graduate student at Yale University. Although a perpetual scholarship kid, he enjoys a well-mixed gin and tonic.

MARISSA "MITZY" WALSH discovered the joys of lacrosse and L.L. Bean blucher moccasins at Pingree School in South Hamilton, Massachusetts, just down the road from Myopia Hunt Club. She did not wear pearls during her time at Smith College, but did learn how to make a mean Cape Codder. A book editor in New York City, her work has appeared in *English Journal, To-Do List,* and her self-published zine, *Indignant Gingham.*